Did You Grow Up With Me, Too?

The Autobiography of June Foray

by June Foray

(with the help of Mark Evanier and Earl Kress)

Foreword by Leonard Maltin

Published in the USA by:
BearManor Media
P.O. Box 71426
Albany, Georgia 31708
www.bearmanormedia.com

ISBN 1-59393-461-0

Book design by Mark Evanier. Cover illustration by Scott Shaw!

This book is dedicated to my husband,
HOBART DONAVAN

and to FAMILY AND FRIENDS
who understood my dedication
not only to my career but to
my love of nature and of
every living creature in
this amazing world.

Left to right: Joe Barbera, Walter Lantz, Don Messick, Daws Butler, the author of this book and Bill Hanna. Five men I miss a lot.

Table of Contents

Here's my star on the Hollywood Walk of Fame – appropriately enough, right next to Jay Ward's. The gentleman with me is Belgian filmmaker Lieven Debrauwer and he seems almost as happy about it as I was.

Foreword
by Leonard Maltin

Like millions of people, I've been listening to June Foray for most of my life. I remember when I first encountered Rocky and Bullwinkle in their first season on TV, and falling under the spell of Jay Ward's sharply-written, wonderfully performed cartoons.

What I can't remember is when I learned that the same woman who provided the voice of Rocky also acted as Natasha, Nell, and a host of other characters on the series, including the gravely-voiced fairy godmother who was patterned after character actress Marjorie Main. But as a diehard cartoon fan, it didn't take me long to memorize the names of the actors in the show's credits (fleeting though they were).

Around the same time I became enamored of Stan Freberg's comedy records, including such hit singles as "St. George and the Dragonet" and classic albums like *Stan Freberg Presents the United States of America*. The rich, colorful voices on those records became permanently ingrained in my consciousness, and in time I connected the dots and realized that June, Paul Frees, and Daws Butler were the same people I heard on so many cartoon soundtracks.

Little did I dream that years later I would get to know the very same June Foray. Appropriately enough, our first encounter was at an animation festival in 1974; oddly enough, it was halfway around the world in Zagreb. I soon learned that as the sparkplug of ASIFA-Hollywood and a longtime member of the Board of Governors of the Academy of Motion Picture Arts and Sciences, June was a tireless cheerleader for animation and short subjects, working to bring recognition to its leading lights.

I think my proudest moment was showcasing June and Bill Scott on a segment for *Entertainment Tonight* in the early 1980s. After I conducted an interview with these old friends and colleagues, I asked if they would be willing to step into our cramped voice-over booth and read through a few pages of an original script from the show. Then I watched them go into action. Within moments, they weren't performers reading lines off a page; they *became* Rocky and Bullwinkle, right before my eyes. The best people in this specialized profession don't simply "do funny voices." They are gifted actors whose talent is too often taken for granted.

June is a buoyant, seemingly ageless person who loves life, and revels in the response she gets from fans young and old. When I was fortunate enough to attend the Oscar nominees' luncheon in 2007, I asked director Martin Scorsese who he was excited to have met that day, among the hundred-or-so contenders and Academy guests. He smiled and said, "June Foray!"

Who wouldn't be excited to meet a living show business legend? Now you can all get to know her better in this long-overdue memoir.

Leonard Maltin

Preface

Talk about being born with a silver foot in the mouth! Through capricious genes, mine was gold. Having discovered the halcyon approach to the birds and bees, I have not only relished living like them, but the *coup de maitre* has been sounding like them.

Like love and marriage, animation and dialogue sound tracks are inexorable compatibles, and yet attempts have been made uncommonly often to proselytize us into believing that animation is solely a visual medium.

Of course, it's visual. So were silent, live-action films with a residue remaining, sadly, of elderly, incurably romantic women-in-black who still extol the wordless virtues of Rudolph Valentino. That mindset was then. This is now. But since Mickey's voice graced our favorite mouse over sixty years ago, audio in animation has been an imperative, especially in cartoons for television.

In 1905, Emile Cohl's puppets should have been so lucky. Film, whether it holds animation, live-action or some new hybrid, reflects life on this planet and those of the extraterrestrials. Bend your ear to the wind. Man, animals, insects and birds are not mutes, and with the imagery of animation, even inanimate objects are endowed with vocal thought processes that are enunciated by facile actors.

Clichéd as it may be, "everyone wants to get into the act" seems to be the way of life these days in the voiceover profession. Nevertheless, no one can be faulted for aspiring to remarkable monetary rewards with a modicum of fame as a concomitant. Also additional perquisites provide each day with new experiences; different casts (although familiar ones are always a joy), scripts (some good, some bad), varied shows, studios who provide the not-so-starving actor with coffee, fruit, sweet rolls and bagels.

As the voiceover profession is constituted presently, the majority of the players have migrated from radio, films, theater, live-action television and comedy clubs. It's obviously a helluva relief for them to simply stand in front of a mike and read scripts without the strain of wardrobe fittings, make-up on the set at 6:00 AM to discipline those encroaching wrinkles, lines to memorize, interminable waits on hot sets. In addition, in animation they can record two or three sessions in a day and make several times the loot. That still doesn't preclude the uninitiated, young restless and talented nor the old and talented for that matter, from hitting it big in a blockbuster animated series. It happens.

Possibly, I have now and then laid an egg, and my producer has been stung, but only by a four-foot-eleven hornet. My symbiotic existence has become the most gratifying achievement of my professional career. Of course, I am female enough to be quite certain that ninety percent of my enthusiasm is resultant of the fact that playing Bugs' love interest is the closest I shall ever come to being a Bunny.

The escapism, characteristic of that Never-Never Land of animated make-believe, has preserved the sanity of audiences for years. Why not actors? Perhaps the role of the performer in the "voice" business is analogous to the sport at the party, who contributes to the merriment of all, including himself, by donning the proverbial lampshade.

Except for one thing. The actor doesn't have to be stoned to appear like a ding-a-ling. For example, where else but in this tangent of show business can a sober adult stand unashamedly before other adults of like sobriety and emit grotesque sounds (animals, birds, insects, inanimate objects, witches, old men, children, seaweed. You name 'em, we done 'em), with accompanying tortured body English and not be reduced to tears of embarrassment?

Impersonations have for some time initiated themselves in the voiceover profession, and it's not singular for a director searching for the voice of an anthropomorphic bat to ask, "How's your Peter Lorre voice? Or Boris Karloff? Or Bela Lugosi?" And there are brilliant actors who can perform those extraordinary imitations. But the rippee (as in, person ripped-off) can't protest. He's dead and couldn't use the money or flattery anyhow.

"For the voice of the bee," suggests the director, "Try a present-day silver screen star!"

Look out! Here comes the friendly Hollywood community lawyer. For those actors incapable of impersonations, too bad! All it does is force them to wait for hours in the unemployment lines practicing to be bees or sons of bees.

Once a way is found into the magic circle of voiceovers, the reality of politics, war, earthquakes, taxes and broken toilets withers. For a couple of euphoric hours, producers, actors, writers and directors live in a fantasy where animal, vegetable and mineral reside side-by-side altruistically and happily ever after in glorious living color, of course.

J.F.

June and the two guys who helped her with this book would like to thank Tiffany Ward, Steven Thompson, Scott Shaw!, Tyler Shelton, Leonard Maltin, Jerry Beck, Denise Kress, Carolyn Kelly, Ben Ohmart, Brian Pearce, Keith Scott, Will Ryan, Dave Nimitz, Sam Spagnolie, Lieven Debrauwer, and June's dog, Shannon for their help.

Me in the early sixties.

CHAPTER ONE

Growing Up,
But Not Much

Springfield, Massachusetts must have changed considerably since my birth eons ago. I wouldn't know, having never revisited it since my family's departure to Hollywood when I was a teenager.

Memories tend to be either selective or elusive. My first ones fall somewhere in between. The earliest recollection of being alive was my standing at the kitchen door screaming for my Mother, who had the audacity to abandon me to hang up wash to dry on the line in the back yard. Reminiscent of Wee Willie Winkie crying at the lock, my head, as I stood there, reached at least one hand below the door knob, my tippy-toes guiding my eyes to the keyhole. I'm guessing because I must have been all of two or three at the time. Coincidentally, decades have not advanced my physical stature much, although life still finds me being a loudmouth – for oodles of noodles, of course. Maybe that's why my Mother, practicing prescient, let me continue to scream.

It was winter and the truck had just delivered the thundering coal in the furnace and the house steamed. It's peculiar how we remember forgettable things and forget important ones. The fol-

14

My mother. She was born Ida Robinson. Very supportive. Extremely
intelligent. My great-great-grandmother was a Mohawk Indian in Quebec
and she married into the Allard family.

lowing recollection is one I wish I could *dis*-remember.

It was about three years after the keyhole incident and I was five, enrolled at Kensington Avenue School in Kindergarten. Since my Father's cooking was considerably superior to Mom's, although both were health conscious before it was fashionable, Bertram, my brother who was three years older, and I gorged ourselves on Dad's scrambled eggs, toast, cantaloupe and Little Orphan Annie's favorite, Ovaltine. The breakfast was naturally nutritious, but something was causing an uneasy rumbling in my tiny tummy. It could have been the heat from the coal-infused furnace or, more likely, the foul-tasting cod liver oil that we had to ingest every morning. Whatever it was that had an adverse effect on me manifested itself even before Mother trundled us into the new Packard to drive us to Kensington, which Bert still attended as well. Being a stoic, I said nothing about my queasiness.

"See you later," my Mother sang out as she drove home to prepare for her bridge club or maybe just to sit at the piano and sing.

Sitting in the classroom trying to concentrate on 1 + 1 and my ABC's, I felt the nausea taking control. The teacher recognized my panic-ridden hand. "Please, may I go to the bathroom?" I squealed. My bladder wasn't full, but my stomach was.

I ran down the corridor attempting to have my short legs win the round over my nausea. Fortunately, they did. My gratitude was also exhilarating because there were no other little girls in the lavatory; so expediently the stall door was left open as I knelt on the cement floor over the tiny toilet. As a five-year old, I had no idea how much a small tummy could hold. I sure found out, though! My throwing-up seemed interminable, and unfortunately for my dietary future, all my mouth could taste was cantaloupe… not even the evil cod liver oil. It wasn't until my thirty-fifth year that cantaloupe could even be tolerated at the same table.

Miss Anthony who taught third grade was the stereotypical schoolteacher at Kensington Avenue School. She was stern with her hair-in-a bun, wearing a simple black dress with sensible shoes.

"Don't you dare misbehave," she warned – as if we ever would have dared. "I'll know because I have eyes in the back of my head."

I presumed that it was my nearsightedness that prevented me

from ever discovering her extra set of eyes, but that didn't prohibit me from looking and examining her head when her back was turned. Too bad that bun was so tight or I might have been able to see something when a stray breeze wafted through.

But bless dear old four-eyed Miss Anthony. She taught us the difference between lie and lay.

"You lie on a feather bed," she said describing the present tense. "You don't lay on it." You could lay on a car horn or you could lay on praise. You could even lay on a nice, thick layer of marmalade while lying on your feather bed, but that would be rather messy. It wouldn't be until years later that I learned what or rather, whom you *do* lay on a feather bed.

There was another teacher in elementary school who instructed us all in different elements of correct grammar, including the conditional tense.

"If I were a tinka, I'd be the very best tinka," she reminded us. I puzzled over this one for some time, but never did ask what a 'tinka' was, nor could I find it in the dictionary. All became clear when I later learned that it was her Bostonian way of saying "tinker." It's fortunate for me that the accent didn't rub off or I might have been forced to become a politician instead of winding up in show business.

They drummed that grammar into my head so hard, or should that be my hard head, that even now, I find myself screaming at reporters who should know better – "WERE" not "WAS." It's "I" not "ME." It's none "IS" instead of none "ARE." Picky, picky, picky, but it seems it's the earliest memories that linger longer. And I'm fine with that. In fact, I rather like it.

My Mother could sing. The birds outside the window turned green with envy as she sang while accompanying herself admirably on the piano. Even in my super-annulations, I can still recite the lyrics of "Come you back to Mandalay, where the old flotilla lay. Can't you hear those paddles chonkin', From Rangoon to Mandalay." At the time I didn't know or care what the Sam Hill "the old flotilla" was, except that to me it represented an exotic, romantic

My brother Bertram and I. I'm about a year old in this and I seem to be studying a script.

world I would later discover in my meandering around the globe. Of course, "You're The Cream In My Coffee" and "Skylark" still spark enchanted dreams of a loving childhood.

Mother and Dad were omnivorous readers. When he wasn't at work, my Father sat in his favorite chair losing himself in classic

Bertram and I again. I'm a little older in this one.

literature or maybe even *Liberty* Magazine. That is, unless he was partaking in one of his other joys, cooking Sunday morning breakfast, Thanksgiving or Christmas dinners.

My Father owned a huge (at least it seemed huge to us kids) auto supply company to bring in the fodder for food. We loved the storeroom in the back where piles and piles of neatly stacked tires gave us almost limitless pleasure jumping up and down, in and out.

The auto supply company was literally a business by which to earn money because in his spare time, my Father was an inveterate, stubborn inventor. Mud Guards were one of his better inventions. He was very proud of those. And so were the powerful auto makers when they later copied his mud guards and called them "bumpers." That was one of his great disappointments and heartbreaks. Since he hadn't filed a patent, there was no way to prove he had come up with the idea, let alone that he'd submitted it to the powers that be in Detroit. In those days, no one would dare take on the auto industry. Although, these days, the auto executives themselves could use some mud guards. Stealing of ideas is not a foreign concept to me when I think of all the plagiarism extant in Hollywood that continues to crush egos and bank accounts.

When I wasn't playing or reading or memorizing or impersonating, I was drawing pictures of Billie Dove and all the stars that I saw in the screen magazines. That and my copying of pictures in *National Geographic*, resulted in Dad's allowing me to draw his advertisements.

Drawing no longer occupies me. However, if I ever find myself with leisure time, oil painting is a surcease from pressure.

The Tate Brothers, influential businessmen, and my Father were dedicated friends. The three of them came up with a fabulous idea, to start the first airport in Springfield. World War I had concluded many years before, and this small town was large enough to accommodate the new love affair with the aeroplane. They developed the airfield and when it was moderately successful, they began holding an air show that would go on to become an annual event. Even Jimmy Doolittle, the first person to fly a plane on instruments alone, piloted his flying machine there.

One time, my Aunt Bert (Wylie at the time) somehow convinced my Mother that I would be safe in an open cockpit with her. I didn't object because I had no idea what I was in for, but the whole concept of flying was exciting. So it was that we took off into the wild blue. She didn't even hold onto me. All I can remember is her laughing hysterically and screaming:

"I'm going to pee in my pants. I'm gonna pee."

I have no idea whether she peed or not, but she was oblivious of the fact that with the impetuous curiosity of youth, I thrust my arm out of the cockpit and felt that it would be severed at the shoulder. That was enough to scare the exhilaration out of me and my relief at landing was considerably more excessive than Aunt Bert's ever was. It would be many years before I got into a plane again.

Mom and Dad were avid theatergoers, hauling the three of us kids – My older brother Bertram, my younger sister Geraldine and me – to the Polis Legitimate Theater or to the X-Movie Theater. No, the X-Movie Theater did not show X-rated movies. There was none back then. It was named for the confluence of intersecting streets. There, I could watch Walter Hampton's *Cyrano* or Eva La Gallienne in her many versatile roles.

I was but six then, old enough to feel the early pains of knowing what I wanted to do with my life (act on a stage as they did) with no concept of how to make that happen at all, let alone soon.

I had been barking at all the dogs in the neighborhood, which probably heightened my vocal acuity beyond my tender years. As is the case with most voice actors, some of my earliest characters were impersonations. I could sound like Mary Boland, Edna May Oliver and Una O'Connor, this last a cockney actress who appeared in many American movies. They got me my first taste of success as my vocal versatility astounded the players in my Mother's bridge club.

If my dream was to be in show business, then my Mother was

My name is Baby June. What's yours?

determined to assist me in achieving that goal. At least, *her* idea of show business.

Eleanor Powell became a famous dancing star in Hollywood; ergo, my Mother reasoned, let us send June to Mr. McKernon's dancing school, which was Eleanor's old alma mater, and *voila*, another but younger rising terpsichorean idol. As unlikely as that was, and even I felt it was unlikely, the bars and mirrors at Mr. McKernon's were graced by a reluctant six-year-old who danced to "Nothing Could Be Fina than to be in Carolina in The Mor-or-horning."

When I was sufficiently trained, it was time for my first recital...in front of Mother's bridge club. Why do Mothers insist on children performing before their "Ladies Clubs?" Presumably, it was to prove that the money they were sinking into the lessons was well spent. Stuffing lamb's wool into pink satin dancing slippers didn't spare me that exquisite pain of pirouetting for hours on my tortured feet.

In retrospect, how unconsciously boring this youngster must have been with her *tours jetés* to bridge players who were impatient not to be trumped. It wasn't all for naught, though, since I can still turn a mean toe to any modern rock band even now.

The weather in Massachusetts during winter is not kindly. Thus, after one of my strenuous dancing lessons, we innocent pupils beat it out into the hall to stand before an open window to relieve our over-heated little bodies. The below-freezing but refreshing blasts put me in the hospital with pneumonia and an abscess on my jugular vein. Well, nothing could be fina than to be in the hospital with pneumonia because it signaled the death knell to my dancing lessons. Good luck, Eleanor Powell with your success. You deserved it.

My next pronouncement didn't meet with the enthusiasm I was expecting: "Mother, I want to be an actress!"

Mother was adamantly opposed. Because of her talent and love of music, the natural progression was piano lessons. Bertram, who inherited that musical gene, sat at the eighty-eights without sheet music and played his little heart and ten fingers out. "Aha," thought my Mother, "June can't contract pneumonia playing piano." And I didn't.

Enter Mr. Dajenais, my patient, suffering teacher who could have commiserated with Professor LeBlanc, Jack Benny's fictional violin teacher. "A dillar, a dollar, a 10 o'clock scholar, what makes you come so soon? You used to come at 10 o'clock, and now you come at noon."

That sardonic nursery rhyme always came to mind because Mr. Dajenais's name always brought to mind the word "Dejeuner," which from French translates to "lunch." I learned that from my French Indian Canadian Great Grandmother.

So, why did Mr. "Dejeuner" come at 4 o'clock in the afternoon? My seven or eight year old mind couldn't comprehend that. Back to piano lessons and the interminable hours of my practicing "In a Country Garden," "Barcarolle," as well as Zez Confrey's exercises. *BO-O-ORING!*

So my fingers hit the keys in random explorations not caring about what had been written on the music sheets. As it would any musician, it irritated my Mother to the point that she would shout from any room in the house, "Sharp! Flat! Sharp! Flat!" Well, that exasperated me. Certainly, this had an even more negative effect on my already deteriorating interest in tickling the keys.

Geraldine was too young to play baseball with Bert, the neighborhood kids and me. She witnessed the "catastrophe" however, when my third finger right hand was broken at the first joint because of my brother's misplaced pitch while I was at bat. Hooray! Disaster strikes again. A gift from Heaven. No more piano lessons. So "Goodbye, Mr. Chips." Goodbye, black keys and white keys and sharps and flats.

Our back yard was graced by a huge maple tree, a ten-foot wall in the rear and a two foot one in the front next to the house. Bert, the would-be juvenile Tarzan, tied a thick rope on a lower limb of the tree and would swing from the rear wall across the yard to the two-foot wall. His friend next door, Edward McNulty, followed suit.

Being the competitive type, I figured that two girls, Edward's sister, Agnes McNulty and I could easily do the same thing. Without the shrill Tarzan whoop, Aggie ascended the tall wall, rope in hand and jumped. Either her aim was off or I just wasn't paying attention, but as I faced the two-foot wall, I felt an excruciating thump on my back. Aggie slammed into my back, pushing me into the wall face forward. *Snap! Crackle! Pop!* There went my right front tooth, broken up to the gum.

Yet *another* catastrophe! Moaning and bleeding, I ran into the house where Mom became hyper-agitated, and with good reason; it was my permanent tooth.

"Oh, my God, oh my God," she shrieked. "Oh, my God!"

Well, God didn't help the exquisite pain I endured having a pivot drilled without the benefit of Novocain. I believe the dentist could have gone on to a lovely career assisting Dr. Mengele, but in any case, to this day, I still get infection after infection, root canal after root canal and bridge after bridge. One thing I do have to thank God for: It didn't affect my speech.

"I keep telling you, Mom and Dad, I wanna be an actress."

CHAPTER TWO

Learning to Talk

Emulating the postmen who defy rain, sleet and dark of night, Geri, Bert and I trudged about three miles every week to the Forest Park library, checking out as many books as each was allowed, those exhilarating classics by Shakespeare, Hugo, Dickens and Chaucer.

They enhanced the myriad of books that Mom and Dad bought for us, especially at Christmas. I even recall getting *Bomba, the Jungle Boy*. My copy of *The Complete Works of Edgar Allan Poe* still remains on my shelf, as do those Elizabethan plays. It's a particularly terrifying thought that if television had been invented at that time, imagine how it would have detracted from those Halcyon literature-packed hours. We did, nevertheless, stop to listen to *Amos and Andy*. Some things are just essential.

As I memorized passages, I would acquire the personas of the book characters in my head. This lead to, I think, developing the vocal and perhaps the intellectual ability to represent them as a performer. I was Queen Guinevere or Lady Macbeth or Titania, Queen of the Faeries.

My first elocution teacher, Miss O'Leary, introduced me to "Little Orphan Annie's come to our house to stay" and rhymes contained in the book *Heart Throbs*, which included Joyce Kilmer's "Trees," and several by Edgar Guest. It was Dorothy Parker with her mordant wit who wrote: "I'd rather flunk a Wasserman test than read a poem by Eddie Guest."

Those were my feelings exactly, which weekly annoyed Miss O'Leary when she discovered that I had memorized "To Lucasta On Going To The Wars" by Sir Richard Lovelace, instead of the detested Guest. "I could not love Thee, dear, so much, loved I not honor more."

There was no doubt about it. We had to upgrade the teacher. The intensive search found Mrs. Elizabeth Larson, a classy, delicate-looking lady, who appeared on the stage with prominent actors like Warner Oland, who eventually migrated to Hollywood and the movies playing Charlie Chan. That was good enough for me and my parents. We had to hand it to Mrs. Larson, because it was she who tempered, honed and professionalized my inherent emerging talent, casting me in plays and ultimately on her radio show at the tender age of twelve. It was at this time when Mrs. Larson said:

"June, I can't teach you anymore. You're better than I am."

Her words, never to be forgotten, instilled enough hubris in me to apply for a professional job. Participating in high-school plays and being voted the best actress in the class didn't hurt, either.

The study of the French language fascinated me, having read Voltaire, Victor Hugo and especially Rostand, whose *Cyrano* devastated me. He was the ultimate sacrificial lamb! Miss McCarthy was the French teacher at Forest Park Junior High, and when I enrolled in her class, I anticipated an exciting adventure, which is exactly what it turned out to be. We translated *Les Miserables* from French into English, much easier than the other way around.

Of course, I identified with Collette. Ah, Miss McCarthy, how indebted I am to you, because my ability to speak French has rewarded me all over the world in my travels, even in Russia.

Mr. Rosenberg, who taught Latin, was my next mentor in a foreign language, albeit a dead one. He was a short, plump man, who incessantly caressed the wart on his nose, and I could never comprehend why he called me "June" when every other student was "Miss" or "Mister." Maybe I was sexy at sweet sixteen.

I guess, in hindsight, I should have asked why I got preferential treatment. But still, Mr. Rosenberg enjoyed the same amount of gratitude I had for Miss McCarthy.

Our class translated "Julius Caesar" with the accounts of battle after battle, not my first antipathy to war, having experienced the feeling while memorizing poems. Even in my senior years, I can still conjugate Latin verbs and decline nouns. With the present world torn asunder, I wonder if all Gaul is still divided into three parts. Poor Hittittes. Poor Huns. Poor Gaul. Poor World. Poor us.

Mr. Fenner, my High school drama teacher, thought enough about my talent to take me to plays. My parents were certainly trusting when they let him "date" me at that tender age. It's easy to forget how much simpler a time it was back then. He never even made a pass. At least it validated my parents' trust.

With Mrs. Larson's guidance and her words in my head and Mr. Fenner's encouragement, it convinced me that I was ready for my professional debut as a member of the WBZA Players at fifteen. Not knowing I was supposed to be nervous, I auditioned for the director, Robert White. Oh, for that naiveté again. Of course, it didn't hurt that I was also blessed with talent.

My New England puritan Mother had never even advised me about the coming of age of a woman. As a matter of fact, on my sixteenth birthday I received a terrific book titled *The Coming of Age in Samoa* by the noted anthropologist Margaret Mead. It mysteriously disappeared the next day. I haunted the bookshops to find another copy, but didn't get to read it until I was an adult.

So, how to hide my innocence and ingenuousness when the cast at WBZA sang the parody of Cole Porter's famous tune, "You're The Tops?"

> You're the tops. You're the breasts of Venus.
> You're the tops. You're the King Kong penis.

Naturellement! I laughed like hell to try, none too well, to veil my embarrassment.

By this time, Mrs. Larson was out of the picture, but she left me with confidence in my acting capabilities. George Bernard Shaw was wacky when he said that youth was wasted on the young, because I was ready. I just didn't know where to go from there.

Perhaps teaching other talented little kids who had the same aspirations. My developing brain cells decided to concentrate on writing material for my one-woman shows in which I appeared before the formerly bored bridge clubbers, who had barely tolerated my dancing, piano and acting recitals over the previous ten years.

It undoubtedly would become wearisome for you to read of my attending summer camp, Brookside Lodge, in the Berkshires, learning to swim, tie square and sheep-shank knots and becoming a woman at the age of eleven, at which time Mother became hysterical, by the way. I must say that it was great sport ice-skating on Porter Lake in Forest Park – not too far from where we lived.

One day, while we were still living in Springfield, Mother and Dad packed my clothes, drove me to a port in New York, deposited me on a cruise ship, which sailed through the Panama Canal and up the West Coast, in order to summer vacation with my uncle Ben Robinson in Los Angeles.

Knowing my intention to continue my career as an actress, his inspiration brought me to the Pasadena Playhouse, where I auditioned and won an appearance in a play, fulfilling my idea to be a stage performer. The director's name was Babette, whose last name I can no longer remember – or the name of the play, for that matter. But Babette predicted a rewarding future for me. My stage and stock plays provided me with all character parts: Maids, old ladies, crackpots, etc…never leading ladies to be kissed by ardent, gorgeous actors. Still, that was the best thing that ever happened to me, especially since I had already accomplished that in radio.

Dad, once comfortably secure financially, lost everything except his loving family in the late thirties. So "Open up those golden gates, California, here we come!" A fortunate transition for him, Mother, Bert, Geri and me.

So, here we arrive in Los Angeles, almost penniless, but elegant, proud and determined. And certainly, my life has been much more intriguing since Los Angeles became home.

CHAPTER THREE

The City of Angels

So there we were in the land of sunshine, orange and walnut groves – nuts of all kinds, even then – Grandpa, Mother, Dad, Bert, Geri and I. We were the genteel poor, groping for incomes, but we had a few things going for us. Mother was a terrific salesperson, the result of being around her father's shoe store for so much of her life. She quickly landed a job at the Broadway department store in Los Angeles, selling footwear to men who were entranced by the exquisite "French" doll.

Dad went into the air-conditioning business, Bert enrolled at UCLA as a psychology major, and Geri signed up for Junior High School, which only left me to decide what to do. I knew what I wanted to do: Acting and writing. But that takes time and the family needed money so I got a part-time job in a drug store for $12.00 a week.

One of the reasons we always needed money was that my parents were generous to the point of lunacy. If they had a dollar and someone needed help, that someone was given seventy-five cents. They were also totally honest in everything they said or did. I'd like to think I inherited both traits.

So it shocked me one day when the owner of the drug store accused me of stealing a hundred dollars. That was a lot of money then...more than eight weeks of my salary. He sent me to make his bank deposit one morning and then later in the day, he confronted me with a stony demeanor, "What did you do with the hundred dollars that's missing from the deposit?"

After crying and denying, I became incensed that I would be accused of misappropriating even a dime. I was devastated, humiliated, mortified, belittled, slandered...pick a synonym and I was it.

Then two hours later, he apologized.

"Sorry, June. My addition was faulty. The entire deposit was intact." Decades later, I still find my heartbeat accelerating at the thought of that moment. Never mind that he gave me a two-dollar-a-week raise to try and make it up to me. Today, I still wish I'd had the vulgarity to say certain words to him and quit. At the time though, my family had great monetary needs and besides, I was seventeen and I didn't yet know some of the words that I now think would have been appropriate.

I knew other words, though. Dad's old Underwood typewriter sat by the alcove in our kitchen, beckoning my ideas, which screamed through my *medulla oblongata* to be released. But first, I needed to do something to begin moving out of the drugstore and into a real career. I called the Screen Actors Guild and joined as an extra at the $25.00 initiation fee. Then I began making calls. In order to get a job as an extra, you needed to call Central Casting, over and over and over until they had something that was appropriate for the person on the other end of the line.

Finally, I got a job. It was as a stand-in to Peggy Ryan, who always seemed to be dancing opposite Donald O'Connor in one movie or another. I don't recall the name of the film or the date. All I know is that I made $25.00, more than enough to pay for public transportation to the job.

By this time, I had learned to sew and make clothes for myself, Mother and Geri. Material then was only fifty cents a yard and if you were small as we were, a dress only required two to two and a half yards of cloth. I think my wardrobe impressed future employers, making them think I was a successful, well-to-do working girl.

That helped and so did a friendship I made during my "extra" period...a young lady named Virginia Mackey. She advised me on every aspect of show biz, not simply radio or pictures.

"You gotta meet Edward Clark," she told me. "He directs his plays at his own theater. He'd love you." That was how Clark entered my struggling life. He'd been a character actor in the movies and a seasoned professional on the stage, and all of that appealed to my eclectic sensitivities. What an exhilarating experience it was, treading his boards, memorizing lines, playing old ladies long before I was one.

Some of the productions were Clark originals but most were those found in the Samuel French catalogues. It inspired me not only to act but to write my own plays, as well. Thus, during my three-month ugly experience at the drug store, I spent much of my time home in the kitchen alcove at the Underwood. There, I wrote a one-act play to be produced at the Wilshire-Ebell Club, a group of professional women, that I had joined because of the focus of the organization, which was on literature, plays and poetry.

I was meeting other actors, getting to know them, swapping tips. From one, I heard that a casting director at radio station KFI was holding auditions. It meant at least an hour bus ride to reach KFI down on Vermont but that was nothing for me then; not if it was going to launch my career as a radio star.

The trouble was I didn't know how to audition. Being a literary classicist, I'd prepared a scene from *Mary, Queen of Scots*. And if they needed to hear more, I had a scene from Eugene O'Neill's *All God's Chilluns*. Great for the stage, wrong for radio. At that time, I didn't know anything about displaying versatility in voice characterizations with colloquial material.

The man in charge was Bud Edwards, a name I'll never forget. He listened patiently to both Mary and the O'Neill piece, then politely but firmly told me to just forget about an acting career. Obviously, he said, I was attractive enough to find a man who'd marry me and support me. My life could be quite beautiful as a housewife and Mother.

I left there furious. All the seething anger I'd suppressed towards my boss at the drug store came bubbling out, redirected at Bud Edwards. How dare he! Pretty much every actor reacts this way at rejection. But more about Mr. Bud Edwards later.

So back I went to that little niche in the kitchen, right in front of Dad's clunky Underwood. It seems like I lived there for months but I must have gotten out. There was still the part-time drugstore job. There was occasional extra work when one of my eight thousand phone calls a week (it seemed) yielded employment. Mostly though, I wrote, always grasping for the new idea that would change my life. Perhaps a live, one-woman evening in the theater or maybe a children's radio show.

I finished the one-woman show idea first. With the few bucks that I earned doing extra work, I rented a little theater on McCadden Street in Hollywood, had programs printed and gave an evening's entertainment to a three-quarter filled house. The admission fee was a dollar, and at least I broke even! The profit was in what it did to strengthen my resolve to be a writer/performer.

I threw myself into the children's show idea with renewed determination. When one is nineteen, as I was in those innocent days, fantasies of classic fairy tales initiate themselves into one's mental processes. At first, mine were all ideas that had been done, done and done to death. However, the pictures of witches, fairies, goblins and elves remain in the psyche – all make-believe. And when I realized that, I had it. I would be June Foray, reading her original stories as Lady Make-Believe. Thus emerged Witch Creakbones, T-Bone Turtle, Hop-A-Doodle, leprechauns, storybook and nursery rhyme people using original plots in stories lasting about nine minutes. If I could sell a fifteen-minute show, it would be ideal for a daily writing chore and the abbreviated thinking span of kids.

I had no idea where to take it. Bless Ma Bell and the telephone directory with all the radio stations listed; radio stations, which had dramatic programming instead of today's rock and talk. I hit pay dirt when I called KFVD, a tiny little station on Western Avenue. The owner's son agreed to put me on air. I guess he thought the price was right: It was free.

Besides, there was another bonus. I had contacted the Los Angeles Board of Education and submitted my scripts, along with the suggestion that my stories could be broadcast into schools as part of the morning curriculum. They liked that idea and of course, KFVD loved the idea of a captive audience. Only days later, Lady Make-Believe hit the air at 10:30 A.M.

Every morning for months, I would take a trolley car down to KFVD, which was a tiny little station on the top floor of an imposing building. Like Superman, I hurled those stairs in a single bound to tell the kids of Witch Creakbones, Theodora the Hippo and Christopher, the boy who always lost himself in the library.

It was an exciting place to be...more exciting than I realized. There was a young man who was also sprinting up those stairs to the station to go on the air with his songs and stories. Maybe it was my lack of sophistication that prevented me from knowing he was already famous and would only become more so. His name was Woody Guthrie.

Another talented man named Byron Dunham read poetry on the air shortly after my program. He said he admired my vocal delivery and asked me to appear with him, reading contemporary and classical poems, which I did. Actually, the readings were the easy part of the performance. Keeping Mr. Dunham's poetic hands off me was the hard part.

There was one thing that was even harder: Trying to get KFVD to start paying me. I never quite managed that part, which is why I left and made a deal with another local station, KMPC, to broadcast Lady Make-Believe each afternoon at 5:30. This job didn't pay either but at least I didn't have to get up so early and spend the day dodging groping poets. Eventually, KECA, which was the NBC Blue Network affiliate, stole Lady Make-Believe away from KMPC by the most devious of all possible means. They offered me money.

It was only $7.50 a week but hey, it was money. A start, at least.

Before long, things were looking up. Allen Joslyn, a casting director at Paramount, converted me from extra work to looping, bringing me in to dub in voices for other actresses. When he discovered I could make the sound of a baby crying, he made special note of that. Mostly, it was a matter of replacing dialogue for some actress who could look good on screen but not talk. There were plenty of those around Hollywood.

Then I had a thought about how to make Lady Make-Believe pay a little better. My show was what they called a "sustainer," meaning that it went on without a sponsor. The station wasn't getting paid for it so I couldn't expect more than the measly $7.50 a week I was getting. But I noticed that immediately before and after my broadcasts, there was always a commercial for Knudsen Milk, and the Knudsen people paid for those ads. I approached Glan Heisch, who was the station manager at KECA and the man who'd offered me the $7.50.

"Mr. Heisch," I said, "would you mind if I contacted the powers that be at Knudsen Creamery to see if they would sponsor Lady Make-Believe?"

With a shrug of his shoulders, he replied, "Try it. It might work." I arranged a meeting for the following week with the advertiser and spent all my time figuring how I was going to talk them into sponsoring my show. I would explain that my only goal in life was to sell truckloads of milk to every child in the greater Los Angeles area. I would mention milk often in my stories and even create new, milk-loving characters who would carry forth the grand message of Knudsen.

The meeting went well, I thought. Two days later, I went in to ask Mr. Heisch if he'd heard from the company.

"I certainly have," he replied. "You obviously did one helluva selling job. In fact, it was *too* good. You're fired!"

Huh?

He explained, "You've built up an immense following in your time slot and that has not gone unnoticed. You see, the man you met with at the dairy...well, his daughter Eleanor Jean has always wanted to be an actress..."

"But...but..."

"He decided he wanted to sponsor a show there that would sell milk the way you described. But he also thought, 'If I'm going to pay for a show, I'm going to give my daughter the job.'"

The next week, Lady Make-Believe was gone. Eleanor Jean was in my slot, telling fairy stories on a show called *Twilight Tales*.

Which explains why I never drank Knudsen Milk again.

CHAPTER FOUR

The War Years

They were unsettling, those between 1941 and 1945 during World War II. When I was nineteen, I was introduced by a friend to a man named Bernard. He worked for a clothing executive at a place downtown in the garment district. Being young and head-strong, I wanted to prove my independence, so I married him. In hindsight, that was the wrong reason to get married, besides the fact that I was much too young.

That he was a jerk also didn't lend itself to a healthy relationship. He would buy clothes leaving us without rent money. We would eat at my Mother and Father's house to save money, so he could spend it on himself. Then he went into the service and he would write home asking for more money, saying, "I don't like the food here. I want to go someplace else." I finally had enough and divorced him after two years.

While our boys were off fighting the war, I fought the battle on the home front in Hollywood. A fifty dollar a month allotment from the government plus twenty-five bucks a throw looping at the studios helped me pay the $49.00 a month rent and to purchase a second-hand Chevy.

All ears were glued to the radio for news of the war in Europe and the Far East. And when we weren't listening to them, we were often tuning in half-hour radio dramas that a man named Joe Micciche was producing for the Office of Civilian Defense. The story-line of each program varied, but they were all about elevating our spirits, assuring us that the war would be won...and won soon.

They inspired me in a couple of different ways. I got to wondering if I couldn't write some of those war dramas. They were far removed from the realm of Lady Make-Believe but I had lots of spare time and plenty of hubris. So I wrote a sample half-hour play, called Mr. Micciche and made an appointment to see him. He read my work, said yes and I had a job, but no pay. They did, however, give me gas rationing coupons so I could fill the tank of my Chevy and get to work. At the time, those coupons were almost as good as money.

I was expected to act as the producer, which meant hiring actors. I turned to Herb Vigran, a well established radio and motion picture actor I'd met at several play readings. He suggested Pat McGeehan as my casting director, an announcer with impeccable years of experience. Pat recruited a number of gifted actors who agreed to perform out of love of country. Not only were they not paid, they didn't even receive gas coupons. Naturally, all the women's roles were taken by yours truly.

Joe Micciche had to assign us to a local radio station, which he did – and so I was foisted upon my old friend, Bud Edwards. You remember Bud, of course. He was the man who advised me to marry, settle down and forget show biz. Here's the letter he received...

February 24, 1943
Mr. John Edwards
Program Director
KFI-KECA
141 North Vermont Avenue
Los Angeles, California

Dear Bud:

Mrs. Hal Berger informs us that she is leaving the second week in March for San Francisco, where she will take a post with the office of war information. She has been writing and casting our "Civilian Defense in Action" program on KFI Fridays at 10:15 P.M.

Beginning March 12th, therefore, we are assigning Miss June Foray, the most talented scriptwriter on our volunteer staff, to the preparation of the KFI scripts. She has been with us since last February, and has been producing some exceptionally fine programs, which have been broadcast by KFAC. She will discontinue her KFAC program and confine herself exclusively to the KFI show.

The show will be cast by Pat McGeehan, whom you probably know as a top-notch AFRA performer.

We would greatly appreciate if you could continue to assign Sid Goodwin to produce the programs.

Also, Miss Foray's scripts will contain many more sound effects and musical cues than those found in Mrs. Berger's scripts. We would appreciate your assignment of a sound-man to the show, such as you did when Hal himself was writing the scripts.

The above, of course, is all subject to your approval, and I trust these arrangements will be satisfactory to you. I would appreciate hearing from you in this respect.

Sincerely,

Joe Micciche

Director, Radio Relations

The show continued until V-J Day and got me into AFRA, the American Federation of Radio Artists. Today, it's AFTRA, The American Federation of Television and Radio Artists.

I worked with many wonderful performers. One was Noreen Gamill, a character actress who recruited me to participate in entertaining the troops. The war's conclusion was imminent, and this was a last chance to contribute by providing a little diversion for some soldiers. Noreen cast me as Sylvia in a production of the Claire Booth Luce play, *The Women*.

We played army bases all over Southern California. Military trucks would pick us up in the afternoon, trundle us off to the camps, then bring us back at midnight. It was rough but it was worth it to hear the laughter and applause of those brave fellows

The Hollywood Canteen. Where servicemen went to meet movie stars and movie stars went to meet servicemen.

who were risking their lives for us all.

Then Saturday nights, we'd go to the Hollywood Canteen, a night club for servicemen that John Garfield and Bette Davis opened up on Cahuenga Boulevard. There were plenty of men there, of course, but not nearly enough women, so that's where we came in. We'd go and dance with the soldiers, swinging and swaying to the music of Kay Kyser and his College of Musical Knowledge. We'd hum along with singers like Ginny Simms and Harry Babbitt or just sit and laugh at comedians like Ish Kabibble. Even Bette Davis was there, acting as hostess. It gave me a certain inspiration to see that even though she was a huge star, she wasn't any taller than I was.

When you're young and dancing all night, fatigue is an un-thinkable concept. That was for old ladies...you know, the ones over thirty. Bringing momentary happiness to men *en route* to the battlefields gave us an additional shot of adrenaline. To all my soldier partners, I lost my heart at the stage door canteen.

In addition to all of this, I was writing for the AFRA bulletins. Before the war ended, the shock of our beloved leader's death in April 1945, devastated all of our citizens. I tried to reflect our collective sorrow in the following article in the May 1945 AFRA newsletter. It was one time when I had to write through my tears...

WE HERE HIGHLY RESOLVE!
AFRA pays tribute to FDR
by June Foray

Democracy has been challenged by a malignant force that would crush the infirm and instill its evil in the hearts of mankind. But the people who have known freedom and the unrestraint of self-government have accepted that challenge and have returned blow for blow, realizing now, at last, the great fruition of their efforts. But even as we in

Entertaining at a USO show. That's me, third from the left: The short one, of course.

America jubilantly hail our fast approaching victory, we bow our heads in grief over the tragic death of our late Commander-in Chief, Franklin Delano Roosevelt.

America is not alone in her mourning, for the name of Franklin Roosevelt burns as a symbol of liberty in the hearts of all freedom-loving people in every corner of the globe. In the most foreboding hours of international chaos, we marched forward in a great coalition against the aggressor with the knowledge that his wise and courageous guidance would lead us to the victory for which United Nations armies on every battlefield of the earth have bled and died.

He died on the eve of our victory, his task of determining the peace unfinished. He is gone, but he has left behind a unified nation steeped in the truths of the democratic way of life. No leader has accomplished as much for the people of his country, for the workers and their unions, for the little man, for the long suffering minorities, for big and little business alike as has Franklin Delano Roosevelt. How grateful we are that he also left behind him plans for an enduring peace, that he taught us that ideals to help determine that peace by ourselves.

Our flags are lowered in sorrow in commemoration of our late President, but our resolve has risen to new heights, the determination to carry on to completion the ideals for which Franklin D. Roosevelt dedicated his life, the determination to stand behind our new President, Harry S. Truman, encourages him to go forward fearlessly and with courage, knowing that he has our support.

As our bells of liberty ring out to welcome our immediate victory, let us be firmly resolved that they shall also toll the death of fascism. We must be united. We must bear the burden of this conflict of ideologies and responsibility of the peace equally upon our shoulders. Franklin Delano Roosevelt has shown us the way. Unity is synonymous with victory. We *will* be unified. We *will* be victorious!

The second world war was over the following August, and I

This is some sort of broadcast or live appearance that has something to do with the Red Cross and the war effort. And I really don't remember anything about it though I know the man at the right is Charlie Ruggles, who was then one of Hollywood's best character actors. A few decades later, he would speak for the character Aesop in the *Aesop and Son* cartoons produced by Jay Ward. We'll get to them later.

was ready to initiate myself into serious radio drama as an actress! Ready for the big time! No more writing. I was eager to make money and buy a new car, *brand* new. Yes, the best was yet to come.

The CBS Radio Building was on Sunset near Gower in Hollywood. Last I looked, it was still there but any day now, it will probably be gone. In any case, it's been a long time since anyone did any radio in there.

The wonderful lobby, I'm sure is long gone. It used to be a large one with comfortable chairs, which accommodated actors seeking artistic employment and afforded them the convenience of nabbing directors and producers as they went by on their way to the individual studios. There weren't any demo tapes – in fact, tape hadn't even been invented. Nor were there any agents, either – not for poor actors, anyway.

So it was up to our courage and brute strength to run and tug at their shirt sleeves, begging for the opportunity to work on their shows. Actors all loved each other and were very helpful in confiding to other actors the places and times of auditions. There were no petty jealousies. It sure isn't that way now!

One glorious morning, typical of California, and despite the paucity of money, I awoke smiling, anticipating chatting with fellow performers at CBS and hoping that I'd find employment that I thought was befitting my talent. Herb Vigran gave me all the know-how and luck was on my side that day... potluck, that is! The Producer of *Pot Luck Party* notified me that I could be assured of at least two shows a week as girl Friday. It was a fifteen-minute sustainer announced by Bob Shannon and starring Jack Bailey, who would go on to find fame as the host of the television version of *Queen For A Day*. At $14 a show, my $49 a month rent and food were guaranteed, along with the $50 allotment I received from the government as the wife of a G.I. Sadly, I became an ex-wife shortly after.

All actors retained a telephone answering service – R.A.T.E., the Radio Actors Telephone Exchange founded by Lou Lauria. Every day we called Marsha Lake to inquire when or if we had a job the next day. Lou, later with perspicacity I might add, published the

R.A.T.E. directory with our photographs. After all, even directors in radio wanted to see what you looked like along with your credits. Marsha endeared herself to the actors and directors by going as far as to suggest casting those with specific talents to the roles required by the directors. It was Marsha who cast me in the role of a lifetime, because I married the writer/director who hired me.

It was one of those lucky days when, feeling the exhilaration of having just performed on *Pot Luck Party* and before hitting the road for my apartment, I called Marsha.

"Any good news?"

"Well, maybe." she said quizzically.

Being aware of my ability to play roles in different dialects, Marsha had recommended me to a producer/director/writer who was new to Hollywood and had seen my picture in the R.A.T.E. directory. My hair hadn't become ash blonde yet, so my picture was most convincing as a Latina, and I had the accent to match.

"His name is Hobart Donavan, and here's his agency number. If you can't reach him there, here's his home phone."

Excitedly, I called him. No answer. He called me. No answer. We went back and forth playing "Dial M for Missed Calls" for almost two days. Finally, his call came through at 8:00 AM.

"This is Hobart Donavan. I'm sorry, Miss Foray, but I've been writing steadily, and I just finished a script for Warner Baxter after working all night." Those were the days of cut and paste with a real typewriter, real scissors and real paste. Remember?

"I hope you're clear for a work call tomorrow."

I was clear and I was ready! Imagine, working with Warner Baxter and at NBC in front of an audience. This job made *Pot Luck Party* look like a potluck party! The trip from my apartment to NBC took about five minutes, since they were both in Hollywood.

The guard at the door gave me the open sesame bit, which led into the hall, off of which the various studio entrances sat. There, at the end of the hall, was the Terrific Triumphant Trio of radio – Dick Ryan, Joe Forte, and Harry Lang, three actors who seemed to be joined at the hip. They were always together on shows or waiting at the agencies and networks for jobs. This may have seemed like a hindrance, but they booked plenty.

"Who in hell is Hobart Donavan?" I asked, and they answered in a chorus.

"One swell guy from Chicago – head writer and director at NBC." It was like a perfect introduction, for just at that second they said, "And here he is now."

Holy Moley! A gorgeous hunk came striding down the corridor, Irish eyes a-smilin'! Do you believe in love at first sight? I did and I do. I ankled up the hall and introduced myself.

"I'm June Foray, Mr. Donavan."

"Yes, I know," he replied abruptly turning on his heels, heading for Studio B.

I must admit to being non-plussed. "Hey, what kind of an S.O.B. is he?"

The rejoinder of the talky trio was "He's fantastic."

Needless to say, Hobe himself believed in that remarkable chemistry of love, because we were married *ten* years later.

Before long, *The Warner Baxter Show*, which was intended as a summer replacement for *Life Of Riley*, bit the dust. Fortunately for Hobe, he'd been writing and directing another show, *Smilin' Ed's Buster Brown Show* starring Smilin' Ed McConnell, that avuncular teller of tales and singer of children's songs. He was also the voice of Froggy the Gremlin and Midnight the Cat. Little did the tykes know that every night, Ed would consume about a pint of Scotch and chase it with many cans of soft drinks, all of which which added to his *avoirdupois*. Still, it kept Smilin' Ed smiling.

In spite of this, every Saturday he'd show up for rehearsal at seven in the morning, sober and professional, with his false teeth securely in his coat pocket. Midway through rehearsal, the teeth were firmly in place in his mouth. And wouldn't you know it, his performances were flawless. What a performer! The show made its debut in Chicago and shortly after, it moved to Hollywood where, fortunately, I was hired as a member of the cast.

Frank Ferrin, the producer, agreed with Hobe's confidence in my versatility, which eventually led to my performing the voice of Midnight, besides playing old Indian ladies, space pirates, ingénues, and all sorts of characters, both good and evil. It amuses me in recollection as I played the space pirate during the show,

Hobart Donavan, aka "Hobe." This photo is from some years later but he was still a pretty darned handsome guy, I thought.

my fellow actors were giggling, almost alighting out loud. Little did I know why. My character had to attack the earthly spaceship, the 'Tiger Shark.' Somehow, when I said that, it kept coming out, "Shiger Tark." I would have broken up myself had I know, in front of an audience yet! My words were repeated *ad infinitum*, Shiger Tark. Oh well, the kids were unaware.

Each filming started the same way. Our announcer, Arch Presby, warmed up the kids, then Ed fired up his theme song and Jerry Maren (as Buster Brown) recited:

"That's my dog, Tige. He lives in a shoe.

I'm Buster Brown. Look for me in there too."

Jerry, who'd once played one of the Munchkins in *The Wizard of Oz*, is one of the "little people," convincing enough for children to believe him to be Buster Brown. He was great to work with, and not just because with him around, I wasn't the shortest person on the set. Jerry was witty and charming...and quite the sophisticate.

When he wasn't working on a movie or TV show, he practically lived at the racetrack.

One Saturday morning before rehearsal, Hobe asked him, "How'd you do at the track yesterday?"

Jerry beamed, "Boy, was I lucky!"

"How much did you win?"

"Nothin'," he sighed with relief. "I came out even."

The show lasted until 1954, when the television version was headed up by Andy Devine and renamed *Andy's Gang*. But before its demise, Alan Livingston, the head Artist and Repertoire man, or "A & R" man, as they're known in the business, hired Ed for a children's album at Capitol Records. This was not only lucky for Ed, but for the rest of the cast since we all went with him. But more about Capitol and Alan later.

In show business, jobs can snowball. You get one rolling and before long, it's like an avalanche. Not long after I'd begun working the Smilin' Ed show, I got a daily – meaning Monday to Friday – series. Once again, it happened in that wonderful lobby at CBS.

Among the actors I'd often see there were the Edwards clan – Jack and Sam Edwards and their sister, Florida. One day, Florida said to me, "Hey, there are two guys over at KHJ auditioning women for a show they're going to do. You oughta go over and try out." I asked her why she didn't do it and she said, "They need someone who can do a lot of different voices. That's you, June, not me."

It was me, so I went over to KHJ and met the two men. One was Wendell Noble and the other was a tall man with glasses. Steve Allen his name was, and as I would soon learn he had an infectious laugh and a wide array of talents. I read for them and they said those lovely words, "You're hired."

That was the good news. The bad news was our time slot. It was a fifteen minute show called *Smile Time* and it aired every day at 7:15. That's 7:15 in the morning. I hate to tell you what time you have to get up when you have to be on the air at 7:15. I'd arrive at the studio at 6:30 sharp and see our live audience lined up, waiting to get in and hear us do the show. And I'd think to myself, "What the hell are you people doing here at this hour? I'm not even sure

STEVE ALLEN

Twenty-Second
April
1 9 9 4

Ms. June Foray Donovan

Dear June,

I've just gotten back from about 87 out of town trips, jazz cruises, concert tours, etc. -- to find your good letter of April 13. What a marvelous break it was that you found those old stories.

In the old days we had Lady Make-Believe. Now the town is full of make-believe ladies.

Sometime within the next few days -- I can't recall the date -- I'm attending some program that concentrates on old-time radio and the Smile Time show is going to be mentioned in that connection.

I also heard Smile Time referred to last week at the Museum of Television and Radio in New York, which has just started a five-month retrospective of my work in radio and television.

As you may know, when I do my comedy concert shows the first half hour is always a total surprise because I answer actual questions from the audience. I don't remember where I was but about two months ago but one of the questions asked about the Smile Time days.

Thanks for sharing with me the earthquake booklet by your sister. It's funny stuff.

All good wishes, June. It's always a pleasure to hear from you.

Sincerely,

Steve Allen

SA/cs

A 1994 letter from Steve.

why *I'm* here and I'm being paid to show up!"

It was a struggle but I was never late. You learn that in live radio and to this day, even doing recording sessions where the world won't end if you breeze in ten or fifteen minutes after the appointed hour, I'm still on time.

Steve was almost always on time...note the "almost." He lived

From many years later: A reunion of the entire regular cast of *Smile Time:* Wendell Noble and Steve Allen, with me in the middle. Steve remained a dear friend for the rest of his life.

down at the beach and there were mornings when he literally ran in with seconds to spare, struggling out of his coat as he did his opening lines. We had one backup in case he didn't make it...one show we'd recorded on transcription disc. If Steve wasn't there at 7:15, they'd put the backup show on and play it until he arrived a few minutes later. Whereupon they'd stop the disc and we'd carry on live as if nothing had happened.

On *Smile Time,* I played everyone and even everything. It was there that I perfected my Spanish accent and where my booming Marjorie Main-type voice got a good workout. I also learned a lot about ad-libbing because there were times when Steve and Wendell would stray from the prepared text and you had to be ready to follow them wherever they roamed.

We did *Smile Time* for two and a half years and there was also an evening version for a while. It was one of the most glorious experiences of my career. Except for the part about reporting for work at 6:30 in the morning.

CHAPTER FIVE

A Capitol Suggestion

Radio had already exposed my versatility to those who hired and fired, but it had never occurred to me to acquire an agent to bargain for higher prices for my voice. It was Miles Auer, my "agent provocateur" who called me. He explained the value of having someone represent you and said he could negotiate a contract with Capitol Records for me to record for their children's albums. That was how Alan Livingston came into my life.

Alan was the A & R man at Capitol. "A & R" stood for "Artists and Repertoire," meaning that he was the main guy to decide who'd record for the label and what they'd record. Alan also wrote a lot of material for the company, especially for their line of kid's records. One of his brainstorms was to create a lovable storytelling clown and to cast Pinto Colvig – an animation gagman and voice actor, along with being a former circus clown – to tell tales. That was how Bozo the Clown was born.

Capitol produced lavish kids' records with large casts of top radio actors, and they employed full orchestras, top songwriters and the best studio vocalists. Some of them, like the Bozo records, were original creations and some of them featured characters licensed from Disney or Warner Brothers. This was in 1949 when records were these brittle vinyl things that spun around on things called turntables at a dizzying 78 revolutions per minute. These

CAS-3080

GEORGE PAL'S

"DESTINATION MOON"

BOZO
THE CAPITOL CLOWN
APPROVED

Capitol
RECORDS
HOLLYWOOD

NON-BREAKABLE

This is the cover from one of I-don't-know-how-many records I did for Capitol. Parents bought them by the ton for their kids..and why not? They were, after all, Bozo-approved.

were the horse and buggy days of technology. No one could have ever conceived of CDs at that time. Some of us didn't even know from television.

It was making those records where I first met and worked with Stan Freberg and Daws Butler, two brilliant performers. The official business office of Capitol was on Vine Street – that famous round building, shaped like a stack of records. It was said that women liked working at Capitol. Some men in the music business like to flirt and there's no way for them to corner you in an office with rounded walls.

We usually recorded in the studio of radio station KHJ down

on Melrose Avenue, next-door neighbor to Paramount Pictures. Alan, a delicious, handsome man, always with an unlighted cigarette hanging from his lips, directed the albums. I can't blame him for being proud as hell in persuading Capitol and Warner Brothers to allow another somewhat well-known actor, Mel Blanc, to be contracted to Capitol.

By that time, Freberg, Butler and I were fast friends who loved and respected each other's talent. Stan and Daws had delightfully wicked senses of humor and we got along great.

In addition to performing for their childrens' records, Stan also got Capitol to let him try some comedy records for an older audience. His first, "John and Marsha" was a strange, funny smash hit. It just consisted of a couple performing a soap opera style scene, saying each others' names back and forth to each other. Stan, who was one of the most versatile voice talents I've worked with, played both John and Marsha.

It was successful enough that Capitol allowed him to follow it with more records. They did well, but it wasn't until he and Daws hit upon a genius idea that the franchise really took off.

Jack Webb was famous on radio for his series, *Dragnet*. It was a cop show delivered in a tight, clipped and serious delivery style. Stan and Daws thought the way the actors talked was hilarious and would be even more so in a different context so they obtained Webb's permission and wrote a parody of it called "St. George and the Dragonet." It was like an episode of *Dragnet* but set in medieval times, with St. George, played by Stan, talking like Jack Webb as he tried to track down a fire-breathing dragon who'd been devouring maidens out of season.

I was asked to play a maiden who'd almost been devoured and I knew I had to deliver something fast. To this day, I have no idea how I came up with it at the last minute, but I did. It was a Brooklyn accent emanating from a maiden almost enveloped by the dragon's breath, a ridiculous anomaly for a sweet Renaissance maiden.

"It was terrible – he breathed fire on me. He burned me already."

For the flip side of the record, we performed yet another *Dragnet* parody, "Little Blue Riding Hood." The announcer, Hy Averback, explained that the color had been changed to prevent an investigation. Those were the McCarthy witch-hunting days and no one wanted to get caught being "Red." So of course, I was Little Blue Riding Hood with a sweet gentle little voice different from the maiden who was almost devoured by the dragon. I was also Grandma.

The record was a phenomenal success overnight. In fact, Capitol had to go to another record company's factory to turn out the thousands needed to meet the demanding sales. It was a best-selling smash in this country but what really amazed everyone was that it hit Number One in Australia. Jack Webb's *Dragnet* had not yet been broadcast in Australia! (A few years later, it made it there. Stan went on a tour down under and people were telling him that someone had plagiarized his St. George record and turned it into a serious cop show.)

One of the many perks of success was that we were asked to fly to New York and perform the record on *The Ed Sullivan Show.* This was back when that series was the cornerstone of Sunday night television-watching. It was practically an American ritual. After Sunday dinner, the family would adjourn to the living room and all watch Ed together.

Stan, Daws, Miles and I met first with Sullivan at his Delmonico Apartment to arrange rehearsal time and become acquainted with this New York T.V. celebrity. We did his show live and the response was so positive that Stan got an immediate call. The producers of *The Perry Como Show* wanted us, and they wanted us the next day. Como had a fifteen minute show every Monday, Wednesday and Friday.

We wanted to do it, and not just for the exposure and money. I wanted to meet Perry Como. He was one of most popular performers in the business, and an old friend of Hobe's from back when my husband was the head writer at NBC in Chicago. Alas, Stan and Daws had a problem. They were still under contract for a daily puppet show back in Los Angeles...*Time for Beany*, produced by Bob Clampett, a former Warner Brothers animator/director. Daws played Beany and his Uncle Captain; Stan was Cecil the Seasick Sea Serpent and the show's dastardly villain, Dishonest John. With

The recording session for "St. George and the Dragonet." The man at left is Walter Schumann, who wrote the famous theme for the *Dragnet* radio show. Jack Webb was nice enough to lend him and the song to Freberg for the parody. Next to him are Stan, Alan Livingston, I and Daws.

In rehearsals with Ed Sullivan: That's Ed, Stan, me and Daws.

those two performing (and often ad-libbing the scripts), the show was a treat, one of those kid shows that adults watched, even if there was no child on the premises.

Clampett had other actors who could sound enough like Stan and Daws to fill in when necessary. Miles got on the phone to see if the fill-ins could fill-in a few days longer. I don't know why but Bob refused. "We need them back here in California as soon as possible." So that's how I didn't get to meet Perry Como.

"St. George and the Dragonet" kicked Stan's recording career into high gear. He followed it with one great comedy record after another, especially after his *Time for Beany* contract expired and he was able to devote himself full-time to recording for Capitol. Some of these were done in tandem with Daws and when there was a role for a female, I'd usually get a call.

One memorable role was that of Bridey Hammerschlaugen, the subject of a record called "The Quest for Bridey Hammerschlaugen." This was Stan's parody of the publicity that surrounded a housewife named Virginia Tighe. She claimed that hypnotic regression had enabled her to recall past lives, including one as a 19th century Irishwoman named Bridey Murphy. (Why Hammerschlaugen? The Capitol Records legal staff was apparently afraid of being sued by a 19th century Irishwoman or something. They made Stan change her last name to something else and he picked one at random out of a phone book.)

Anyway, in the record, Stan hypnotized me and took me back to some past life. In retaliation, I took him back to a past life... and he turned out to be Davy Crockett. Mr. Crockett was then the biggest thing on TV and kids everywhere were sporting coonskin caps. I told him it was too bad he wouldn't be around in my era to cash in on the craze...to which he responded, "How do you know? In my next life, I could be Walt Disney."

Stan was a brilliant satirist but a demanding boss. He would do take after take to get what he wanted, and it was not uncommon for him to make us do the material seventy or eighty times...

...and then, of course, he'd use Take #2. But I still love him.

Another problem was that Stan was and is a night person, the opposite of my little diurnal self. He liked to record at night and the way he worked, that sometimes meant we wouldn't be done until the wee hours of the morn.

One time, he set up a recording session at 8:00 P.M. at the new Capitol Records round building on Vine Street in Hollywood. It was one of the few times in my career I can recall having a scheduling conflict that caused me great consternation.

I had a session that same evening with Jay Ward, Bill Scott, Daws Butler and Edward Everett Horton to record five *Fractured Fairy Tales* for *Rocky and His Friends*. I recorded two stories and told Jay that I had to run. I begged him to let me pick-up my lines another time.

Jay felt bad, but he just couldn't as he needed the tracks that night, so he had to expeditiously hire another actress. I rushed to Capitol to be on time for Stan at 8:00. I'm sure you've already guessed the punchline to this story. Stan was late and I could have recorded the other three *Fractured Fairy Tales*, which, as produced, turned out to be less comedic and sharp. Oh well, that's how the microphone crumbles.

It was late that night by the time we finally started and before I knew it, it was 2:30 in the morning and we still weren't finished. I don't know if I woke him or not but I called Hobe about 3:00 AM, knowing that he knew that I was still working with a professional, decent fellow, Freberg, and not trysting. The sun had already risen when I trundled along home at 7:00 in the morning, took a shower and hit the road to a rehearsal for a radio show. Yes, radio. The theater of the mind was still alive and well, not yet finished off by the box called television.

Even after our contracts with Capitol concluded, my association with Stan continued. In 1957, the great Jack Benny retired his long-running, legendary radio program and moved exclusively into television. He'd been doing both for several years but when the time came to give up on radio, CBS went looking for a new comedian to take over Benny's coveted time slot.

They picked Stan and then Stan picked Daws, Peter Leeds, a singer named Peggy Taylor and myself to be the regular cast of *The Stan Freberg Show*, the last network comedy radio program of that classic kind. The show was without fear and without equal. It was also, unfortunately, without sponsorship. Few companies wanted to put their money into that kind of program any longer.

One that did was American Tobacco but Stan, ahead of his time, had decided cigarette advertising was not healthy for human beings and other living creatures. He told CBS to try and find him a sponsor whose product didn't kill people. Well, they never did, which is why *The Stan Freberg Show* only lasted fifteen weeks.

While it did, it was enormous fun, working with him and Daws and Peter and Peggy. He had Billy May doing the music and Jud Conlon's Rhythmaires to supply vocal stylings. We did it each week in front of a live audience at that CBS studio on Sunset Boulevard, the same one where I used to sit in the lobby and

Peggy Taylor, Stan Freberg, Peter Leeds, me and Daws Butler.

wait for auditions. I was cast in all sorts of roles but my favorite was probably Miss Jupiter, an interplanetary beauty queen. I don't know what she looked like – everyone made up their own picture of her in their imagination – but she said she was two feet tall with shapely wheels.

After the lack of sponsorship ended the show, Stan continued to make records. I was proud to be in his 1961 masterpiece, *Stan*

Same people. Different seating arrangements.

Freberg Presents the United States of America, Volume One, which some have called either the most historical funny record ever made or the funniest historical record. Stan promised me I'd be in *Volume Two* and he kept his promise, even though he didn't get around to recording it until 1996. At this rate, I expect to get a call for *Volume Three* some time around March of 2031.

In between volumes, Stan also did other records but he mainly turned his formidable talents to producing commercials. Most of them were a lot more entertaining than the shows they interrupted. Every now and then, I work in one of his projects and it's always a joy to get those calls.

Alan Livingston continued to thrive at Capitol Records. His standing improved a great deal when he suggested the company sign a largely unknown band called The Beatles. It's hard to believe that both Bozo and Ringo owe their careers to the same man. Eventually, Alan went off into television and film production. He was one of the people responsible for the smash TV series, *Bonanza*, as well as several successful feature films.

For a time, he was involved with an animation studio called Pacific Rim. He kept calling Stan and me about providing voices for its productions but as too often happens in our business, someone decided to do things on the cheap. It costs less to record cartoons in Canada.

I don't know how many times this has happened. Someone

Between jobs, I could often be found at the Brown Derby restaurant near Hollywood and Vine. And when I wasn't there, my caricature was. That's it right above me, next to Stan's.

starts out wanting to do the best show or movie possible but the money guys begin squeezing the budget, and the next thing you know, they're looking to save a few bucks by recording voices in Toronto or Vancouver. Alan called a couple times to apologize to me that they'd had to do this.

He was a dear, dear man and I felt awful when I heard that his son, whom I met when he was a child, died at the horrifyingly-early age of 40. He was a hemophiliac and had received a blood transfusion containing the AIDS virus. Sometimes life isn't fair. Other times, it's *really* not fair.

Alan passed away in March, 2009. I didn't get to see him the last few years but I'm certain he was still the same handsome hunk at the age of 91 as he was in the fifties and sixties.

Something else interesting happened to me in the mid-fifties, I got married again, this time for keeps.

From the moment I'd first met Hobart Donavan at that radio show, I knew that I was destined to be with him. I'm not claiming to be psychic. It was just an instinct. And maybe I can be accused of being a romantic because it truly was love at first sight.

I had gotten divorced from my first husband in 1945, but Hobe's wife, who was a staunch Catholic, refused to grant him one.

In the meantime, we lived together for eight years while waiting for his wife to give in. She never did but eventually, Hobe was able to divorce her.

In 1955, we took out a marriage license, but the Judge was too busy that day and then I was working all the time. It had been eight years already, so there didn't seem to be any particular rush. The license just sat around, waiting for the right moment.

The moment happened a few weeks later while I was working with Frank Capra. Yes, the Frank Capra from *It's A Wonderful Life* and *Mr. Smith Goes to Washington*. He was doing live-action educational films for the Bell Telephone Science Series, starring Dr. Frank C. Baxter. There were animated inserts and Saul Bass, who'd been hired to produce them, recommended me to Mr. Capra.

Anyway, I had been working on one and as soon as I had finished for that day, I called Hobe, who was working at home, to tell

Mr. and Mrs. Hobart Donavan. Taken at the Magic Castle in Hollywood.

him I was on my way there. Out of the blue, he said, "How would you like to get married?"

Of course I wanted to, but where would we go? It seems that Hobe had been busy researching a wedding locale rather than researching his latest project. He had called all over town and met with a lot of resistance. "Oh, well, you have to have flowers and you have to have guests," they would tell him. Apparently, just having two people who were in love and wanted to spend the rest of their lives together was insufficient for a wedding.

Hobe said, "I finally found a place. You've gone past it a million times. The Little Brown Church on Coldwater Canyon." I knew it very well.

We got to the church and a young man greeted us, "Unfortunately, the minister has a very bad cold. Would you mind going over to his house?" We didn't and we did. Didn't mind and did go to his house, that is. The minister's wife acted as the witness. It was a perfunctory service, but it did what we needed it to do and we were married.

A few years later, my sister Geri married Sam Spagnolie at the very same Little Brown Church. The very same minister came out, looked at Hobe and said, "I know you." Then he looked at me quizzically and added, "But I don't know *you!*"

Hobe remarked, "How could you? She had a handkerchief over her face crying the whole time!"

There is one disappointing element to the story, but I knew it going into the relationship. Hobe had a two-year-old son who drowned in a swimming pool. Then his other son suddenly died of a heart attack in his twenties. He also had two daughters. When we got together, he said, "Please, June, I don't want any more children." I had to respect his request. I wish I hadn't, but I did. It's one of my only regrets in life.

CHAPTER SIX

Getting Animated

Radio was great. Everyone who worked in radio misses radio, at least the way we did it. Those of us who worked worked all the time and it was not uncommon to do three or four different shows a week – and why not? You didn't have to memorize lines or be fitted for costumes. Audiences couldn't even get sick of your face because they never saw your face. If you could sound like six different people, you might as well be six different people. At least as far as the folks at home were concerned.

I played romantic leads, childrens' parts, comedy relief side-kicks, little old ladies, sultry vamps, everything – sometimes several of those, all in the same show. I did comedy shows, kids' shows, dramatic shows, mysteries. At times, the biggest mystery was "Where do I have to be?" And more important, "When?"

At times, it felt more like a series of parties than employment. If the show was on at, say, 8:00 that meant we had to do it twice – once at 5 PM as a live broadcast for the East Coast, then again three hours later for the West Coast audience. In-between, the cast and staff would often repair to a nearby watering hole for food and beverage. At times, one or more performers might consume a bit too much beverage and it would make the second show funnier. Or at least, it might seem that way to us.

Once on an evening show I did for CBS with Steve Allen, we

Here I am on some radio show or other with Dennis Day, who was so popular on Jack Benny's program.

had a guest actor consume way too much grape at dinner. He was babbling along as the rest of us frantically searched through our scripts, trying to find some trace of what he was saying and our lines to utter in response. Steve was the first to figure out that we were on a runaway train and the script was inoperative; nothing being said resembled anything that had been written.

If it bothered Steve, he didn't let on. He just dropped his script and began ad-libbing in response, making it up on the spot. It turned out to be a pretty funny episode and it demonstrated the kind of talent that would stand Steven Valentine Allen in good stead just a few years later. That was when he would start *The Tonight Show* and invent so much of what we know now as late night television.

I worked with some people of great talent and stature, sometimes both. My first national radio show was on November 1, 1943 – a dramatic anthology called *Cavalcade of America*. It was an episode called "The Burma Surgeon" and one of the other thespians involved was a wickedly witty gent named Hans Conried. I would later spend much of my life sharing recording studios with Hans, always to my great pleasure.

There were shows with Jimmy Durante and Phil Harris and Edgar Bergen and Danny Thomas. One time, I was cast in a radio version of the Bob Hope movie, *Ghost Breakers*. To play the Bob Hope role, they made a wise choice and got Bob Hope.

I was pretty young at the time but they had me playing some odd, older characters. In this case, it was a voodoo woman who only had a few lines but I gave them all I had, and the audience howled. Bob walked over, gave me a kiss and then he said into my microphone, "Hey, I thought I was the only one here who had any funny lines."

Before long, I had a pretty good reputation for being reliable and being a lot of different people. I think I was working on *The Phil Harris Show* when I got the call to go do something called *Speaking of Animals* for a producer named Lou Lilly.

Speaking of Animals was a popular series of shorts that ran throughout the forties and into the fifties. They were not exactly cartoons but they were not exactly not cartoons.

They looked like little documentaries about animals. Lou had a crew that would go out and shoot footage at zoos or in the woods and then you'd hear a serious narrator tell you about the lovely creatures. He'd be telling you about the lifestyle of a penguin and how these aquatic, flightless birds could endure the most chilling of temperatures without so much as a care –

– and then on screen, you'd see the penguin say, "I don't care what anyone says. I'm cold!"

That was why they called it *Speaking of Animals*. The animals spoke.

It was live-action footage but what they did was to animate mouths and superimpose them over the real animals' mouths or beaks or whatever they had. And sometimes the voice you heard would be one of mine. (Sometimes, it was another talented radio performer named Stan Freberg but I didn't meet him just then. All

I appeared several times with Arthur Godfrey (center) when he was the biggest star on radio *and* TV. The other gentleman is Jerry Hausner, an actor who also perfomed and directed cartoon voices, mainly for the Mr. Magoo films produced by UPA.

Lucifer the Cat from *Cinderella*. © Walt Disney Productions.

the actors were recorded separately.)

It was fun doing *Speaking of Animals*. I only had a few lines in each one so I could be in and out in twenty minutes.

Then Disney called. I don't mean Walt himself. I mean the studio. Since I worked for the studio many times while he was alive, people always ask me what he was like. They're disappointed, and so am I, that I have to tell them I never had the pleasure.

But I met his casting people and directors. They'd heard me on radio and in childrens' records I was making and had me in several times to audition for this or that, and I wound up playing the role of Lucifer the Cat in *Cinderella*. Shortly after that, Tex Avery began using me for voices in the hilarious cartoons he was directing over at MGM.

Disney – again, the studio not the man – had me back to voice Witch Hazel, the first in my long string of animated witches, mostly with that name. It was for a popular Donald Duck cartoon entitled *Trick or Treat*. I did a lot of cackling and shrieking as I menaced poor Donald and his nephews. I was also cast as an Old Squaw in the

Disney version of *Peter Pan.*

It was a few weeks after I'd recorded the Old Squaw role that I got a call from Jack Lavin, Disney's casting director, to report to the studios for another job in the same film. Oh, and by the way, "Please bring a bathing suit."

"A bathing suit!?"

Well, with some casting directors, I might have worried what he had in mind. But this was Disney so I packed my bathing suit and reported as ordered. What they had in mind, it turned out, was for me to play a mermaid for purposes of Rotoscoping.

Rotoscoping was a technique that dated back to the days of silent cartoons when the Max Fleischer studio employed it. Someone would put on a clown suit and then perform the actions that Koko the Clown was to perform in the cartoon they were making. The film would then be projected into a special drawing table and traced, frame by frame. The animators' drawings would be based on those tracings. They might follow them closely or just use them as a guide but either way, it helped, especially when animating a character with realistic human proportions.

A lot of studios didn't employ it, either because they didn't have the need or, more often, the budget. But Mr. Disney, that man I never met, had a "spare no expense" attitude about the making of cartoons. He hired me and two other actresses, Margaret Kerry and Connie Hilton, to be filmed as reference for the mermaids in the film. Margaret also played Tinker Bell for the camera.

We put on our swimsuits and then each of us had her feet tied together. For a couple of hours, we had to writhe around on little boxes and platforms that stood in for the rocks the mermaids would be on. Then finally, someone said, "Thank you" and they untied my feet and let me go home.

A lot of people would later credit me as having performed the voice of one of the mermaids but that wasn't I speaking. Disney did sometimes use the voice actors in that capacity. For the same film, Hans Conried not only spoke for Captain Hook but was filmed for Rotoscoping purposes, as well. But I just played the Old Squaw and later let them tie my feet up.

A scene from *Andy's Gang,* the television version of *Smilin' Ed's Buster Brown Show.* The Indian in the center is Lou Merrill and I wish I recalled who the other actor was.

By that time, I was starting to realize that I belonged at a microphone, not in front of a camera. But every so often, I let myself get dragged where I didn't belong. One time, it was by Frank Ferrin from *Smiilin' Ed's Buster Brown Show* and *Andy's Gang* who got me there...for a lowest-of-budget 1954 dramatic movie called *Sabaka*. It was kind of like what *Gunga Din* would have been like if *Gunga Din* was filmed at the 99-Cents Store, featuring most of the cast from his radio and TV show except for Froggy the Gremlin.

The lead character was Gunga Ram, a young elephant trainer whose sister Indria and her husband were murdered by the leaders of a religious fire-cult. Bored already, aren't you? Gunga Ram swore vengeance against the cult and vowed to destroy it, despite the opposition of the Maharajah of Bakore and his military commander, General Pollegar. And I'm not sure what happened because I haven't seen the film in half a century but I think Gunga Ram triumphed. At least, I hope so.

My role? The exotic, romantic lead...Marku Ponjoy, High Priestess of Sabaka. If you are at all a fan of me, do us both a favor and don't track down a print. Years later, when I became involved with the Board of the Academy of Motion Pictures, I tried to convince their Preservation Department to transfer all the remaining prints of *Sabaka* to flammable Nitrate stock.

But it was fun to make, especially because of the other actors. The Maharajah of Bakore was played by a dear character actor friend named Lou Krugman, who had about as much East Indian blood in him as I did. And General Pollegar was portrayed by Boris Karloff, who was pretty charming for a guy who played some of the roles he'd played.

Sabaka and one other job for Frank Ferrin pretty much ended my career on-camera, at least for a while. The other one I can barely remember but it called for me to play a young woman fighting for her life with a phony squid. That might have been fun, had it not required being in the freezing water for at least three hours. Sure, it's warm in Southern California...but not in the Pacific Ocean in the middle of winter.

Were the pain and suffering worth the hundred bucks? When

Marku Ponjoy, High Priestess of Sabaka.

Still Marku Ponjoy, High Priestess of Sabaka. This was three years before I began playing a more natural role: A flying squirrel.

it was my only source of income, probably. But as more and more voiceover and radio jobs came my way, I started to realize I was more comfortable leaving the on-camera jobs to others. I spent less time auditioning, more time performing. The range of roles I could play was also not as limited. In front of the camera, I could only really portray 4'11" women in my age range. At the mike, I could be a little girl, an old witch, a giantess, a pussycat, whatever. Best of all, when you work in voiceover, you don't have to get into sub-zero water with a rubber octopus.

Even as the radio business was declining, my cartoon work was picking up. In addition to working for Tex at MGM, there were calls from Walter Lantz, whose studio produced the Woody Woodpecker cartoons. Woody had a niece named Knothead and a nephew named Splinter, and from time to time Walter would have me come in and put words in their beaks...or have me play some other character he and his gagmen had concocted.

There were also, happily, the Warner Brothers cartoons. I became the voice of Granny, the saintly but feisty owner of Tweety and Sylvester in the films directed by Friz Freleng. I played a mouse who reminded you of Audrey Meadows in the "Honeymousers" cartoons that reminded you of the *Honeymooners* TV show. Robert McKimson directed those.

I did an awful lot of jobs for that studio and so did other actors who would soon be or were already my co-stars on many projects...

This is I on some early TV show. I have no idea what the show was or who that man was.

One of the "Honeymousers" cartoons. I played the Alice mouse while Daws Butler played the mice who sounded an awful lot like Jackie Gleason and Art Carney. © Warner Brothers Cartoons.

men like Daws Butler and Stan Freberg. But you wouldn't know it to read the credits. Mel Blanc, who was the main voice actor for WB, had this very special contract. Somehow, no matter how many of us were also in the cartoon, Mel's was the only name mentioned.

That didn't bother me a lot then and it only bothers me a little now. So much of my career has been anonymous, dubbing in voices for other actors or speaking in commercials with no credits whatsoever. The Warner Brothers cartoons were so iconic and enduring that it was an honor to make even an unbilled contribution.

How did I start working for them? Well, it all began with a guy named Jones. Let me tell you about him...

CHAPTER SEVEN

Chuck Who?

One morning, my agent Miles called and asked, "June, do you want to work at Warner Brothers tomorrow?" Like I was going to say, "No, I'd rather wax the kitchen floor."

I had never been called by Warner Brothers before. He said, "You're working for Chuck Jones."

To which I replied, "Chuck who?" I didn't know who that was. Then.

He said, "Jones. He does a lot of the Bugs Bunny films." Okay, Bugs Bunny I knew. But who was this Jones person? Funny how one day you've never heard of someone and the next day, they're one of the most important people in your life.

So the next morning, I drove up to the Warner's gate in my brand new Cadillac and the guard had my name, just like he'd probably had Jimmy Cagney's name or Humphrey Bogart's before me. You couldn't drive onto that lot and not think of things like that. I was directed to Projection Room 14 where I was met by a tall, gorgeous man with an effervescent smile. The man and the smile were Charles M. "Chuck" Jones, already well on his way to becoming one of the most respected cartoon directors of all time.

"You know, I've been waiting to meet you for a long time," he said. And I guess I'd been waiting to meet him for a long time even if I didn't know who he was.

Behind him was a little man with a moustache. He was jocular and he was pleasant. He was also Mel Blanc, the voice of Bugs Bunny, Daffy Duck, Porky Pig and so many other already-legendary cartoon characters. Mel could do any male voice a producer needed and he could even play a woman on occasion. If he'd been a bit more versatile with his female voices, they wouldn't have needed me there. I'd been waiting a long time to meet him, too.

We chatted for a while and it was all very pleasant and all very exciting for a young gal just starting out in the animation industry. I hadn't worked for anyone except Disney at that point.

I have a photo of that moment and it's at the bottom of this page. A man named Treg Brown took it and as I later learned, he was the genius behind the great sound effects and editing in the Warner Brothers cartoons. As I look at that picture today, I'm appalled – not at how young we all are but at the cigarette dangling from my hand.

We all smoked then. Mel smoked a lot and it almost seemed like a requirement of the job. Most of the radio shows then were sponsored by cigarette companies and if you were performing on a Lucky Strike show, they expected to see you puffing a Lucky Strike

Me, Mel Blanc and Chuck Jones...the first of many, many times we'd work together. Photo by Treg Brown.

all through the rehearsals. It wasn't until 1964, when I thought Rocky the Flying Squirrel's voice was beginning to deepen that I finally quit.

I don't think Mel ever gave it up. For years and years, through hundreds of sessions where we worked together, he was always smoking away like a chimney. Once I gave it up, it began to bother me. In the mid-eighties, I was doing a guest shot on a revival of *The Jetsons*. I was working a microphone to Mel's right and he had a cigarette burning away in his right hand. As Rocky would say, "Hokey smoke!" Suddenly, I found my lungs filling with nicotine.

As politely as I could, I asked him to knock it off. Mel just shrugged and transferred the cigarette to his left hand, inflicting it on Jean Vander Pyl, who was doing the voice of the Jetsons' robot maid on the next mike over. I guess it didn't bother her but it bothered me. It bothered Mel too, though he didn't seem to notice. The last few times we worked together, he arrived at the session, dragging his oxygen tank on a little two-wheeled cart.

Also in the photo, I see I'm wearing glasses. My being near-sighted in one eye and farsighted in the other had caused my Mom to worry, thinking it was a brain tumor or something worse. A nice ophthalmologist fitted me with corrective lenses but as I found out later, I didn't really need them. A few years after that, my brain adjusted and off came the glasses. Even today, at age mumble-mumble, I can read the fine print on the Vodka labels and see Rodeo Drive six blocks away.

Back to my first day at Warner Brothers.

As I was chatting with Chuck and Mel, a man came over and introduced himself as Mike Maltese. He was the storyman who thought up the plots and gags for most of the 1950s cartoons Chuck directed. As we shook hands, he said, "You're a Virgo," Naturally, I was taken aback. He also informed me that my I.Q. was superior to the average, and I thought, I'm going to like this man.

I liked Chuck too, right off the bat. He chimed in and said, "Hey, I'm also a Virgo. I was born September 21." I was born on the 18th, and from that day forward, until he left us for "Upsida-sium," Chuck and I always exchanged mutual birthday greetings every year.

He was, I came to learn, the intellectual of the animation world, wont to quote Mark Twain at the drop of a pegboard. One of his favorites was Twain's observation that "Fewer things are harder to put up with than the annoyance of a good example." That certainly didn't pertain to Chuck or to the film we were about to record – a Bugs Bunny short called *Broomstick Bunny.* He handed me a script and I looked to see what my role was and...

I couldn't believe it: Witch Hazel. Another witch named Witch Hazel, just like I'd played for Disney.

Oh, this one looked completely different. But she was a witch and she was named Hazel and she was going to sound like me and she was going to do to Bugs pretty much the same things the other Witch Hazel had done to Donald Duck.

Some people won't get the name today. Witch Hazel was a product you could buy in stores – very popular then, not as popular now, although you can still buy it at Walgreen's. It's an astringent used for cleaning the skin, and both my witches were named for it. But I'll bet you kids see it on drugstore shelves and think, "Hey, they named that after the green lady in the cartoons." (Just before he passed away, Marc Davis – one of Disney's wonderful "nine old men" – told me they'd mainly named their Hazel after a beloved nurse on the studio lot.)

Since neither studio really owned the name, and people weren't as litigious as they are today, nothing was said about the duplication of witches. You see, back then, no one really expected the films to be seen much after they played theaters for a week or two, which was short-sighted in both eyes. They were wonderful cartoons and they deserved to be seen again and again, by generation after generation.

Chuck Jones turned out to be the perfect director for my kind of voice actor. It's refreshing and constructive not to be over-directed or to have the guy in charge giving you line readings, performing the copy the way he thinks it should sound and expecting you to imitate him. Hire the right performer and you get the right performance. Chuck believed in that. I wish more directors did.

Mel waited while they recorded me first. Years later on most

TO JUNIE —
WHO HAS MADE SO
MUCH OF ME POSSIBLE
ALL
MY LOVE

CHUCK JONES -1977
© WARNER BROS

Chuck Jones was always so generous with his wonderful drawings. I'd see him at animation events, mobbed by adoring fans, shouting out, "Please...a Road Runner!" Or "Please...a Pepe LePew!" He'd stay as late as it took to please everyone. Or if he couldn't stay, he'd take their addresses and three days later, they'd have their treasured sketches in the mail. © Warner Brothers Cartoons.

TV animation, actors were recorded in a group, much like doing a live radio play. But in theatrical animation, the custom was (and in most cases still is) to record one actor and then another. In fact, if you were playing multiple roles, you'd usually record one character's lines for the entire film, then go back and do another's. Mel, doing a Tweety and Sylvester cartoon, would sometimes record Tweety one day, then come back the next to play the Puddy Tat.

I did my first line as this Witch Hazel, then waited for Chuck to tell me to do it again – faster, slower, louder, whatever. Instead, to my surprise, he moved on to the next line.

"Don't you want me to do it again?" I asked.

He said, "No, that was fine."

And that was how it was with Chuck. He knew what he wanted – or at least, he recognized when he had something good – and that was it. On to the next.

In the years since, I worked for a great many directors who didn't know what they wanted. Not so with Chuck. Not in all the many years we worked together after that.

I had seen but not met Mel "The Man of a Thousand Voices" Blanc in the corridors at NBC and CBS, scurrying from one radio program to another. He was on so many shows, there were times he had to be in three rehearsals at the same time and Mel, being Mel, darn near made it.

After I left, he recorded his Bugs Bunny lines. When I saw the finished short months later, I was astounded. Bugs and my Witch Hazel chatted so naturally, playing off one another, you'd never have known we hadn't been recorded at the same time.

It was also a very funny film, one that most people seem to remember quite well. Witch Hazel was a crazy, clunky thing, reveling in her basic ugliness and determined to stay that way forever. Bugs switched around some potions she'd poured into teacups and she was transformed. A man in a mirror (also voiced by Mel) informed her she wasn't so hideous anymore.

She was amazed at what she saw in the mirror. I was amazed at what I saw on the screen.

It was a real cartoon – a very good one – with my voice coming out of a wonderful, memorable character. And Chuck had even designed her with a little bit of me in mind. That was how I wore my hair back then.

The two Witch Hazels were my first two witches but far from my last. For a while, it seemed like half the directors in town were saying, "Let's get that little lady who does the witches." When Bill Hanna and Joe Barbera were directing Tom and Jerry cartoons for MGM, they had me do one in a short called *The Flying Sorceress*. Years later, I played Broom-Hilda, the comic strip character, for Lou Scheimer's Filmation Studios and there were all those witches in the *Fractured Fairy Tales* cartoons for Jay Ward, and so many more. I sometimes felt like I should be arriving at the recording sessions on a broom.

But what's interesting is that I can't recall ever playing a truly nasty witch, the kind you long to see melted into a puddle or shoved into an oven. My witches were sweet, funny and sometimes a little dotty. Even then, I 'm lucky I got out of Massachusetts. You know what they used to do to witches up in Salem.

When I got home that night from working at Warner Brothers, I thought that it was nice, but I presumed it was my last time working with Chuck Who? I wound up doing hundreds of cartoons with that incredible animator, writer, producer, director and dear, dear friend.

Chuck was an amazing talent. In his lifetime, he made more than 300 animated films and won three Oscars, plus he was awarded an honorary Oscar in 1996 for lifetime achievement. I don't know anyone who achieved more than Chuck.

Charles M. "Chuck" Jones was born, like he said, on September 21. The year was 1912. The place was Spokane, Washington. But he grew up in Hollywood, watching Charlie Chaplin and Buster Keaton film their classic comedies, absorbing the whole dynamic of funny people moving in funny ways and doing funny things.

He went to Chouinard Art Institute in Los Angeles, drew cartoons for money downtown on Olvera Street, and eventually got into animation when Ub Iwerks – the legendary Disney animator, now off on his own – hired him as a cel-washer. That meant that after the cels were photographed, Chuck washed the ink and paint off them so they could be used again.

That year was 1932. He worked his way up from taking the drawings off the cels to putting them on. Then in 1936, he was hired as an animator at the Leon Schlesinger Studios, which eventually became Warner Brothers. He worked with directors Friz Freleng, Bob Clampett and Tex Avery and directed his first cartoon in 1938.

The first few were good but not great. The great came later. All those years of studying the great clowns paid off for Chuck. He had the timing of a master. Before long, he was directing cartoons with his distinctive style and pace. *One Froggy Evening. Duck Amuck. Duck Dodgers in the 24th and a Half Century.* All the good Road Runner and Coyote cartoons. And so many more, including some of the best Bugs Bunny shorts like *Rabbit Seasoning* and *What's Opera, Doc?*

Apart from a brief stint at Disney, Chuck stayed there, directing some of the finest cartoons ever made, until the W.B. Studio closed down in 1962. Then he moved over to MGM, where one of his first assignments was to do something about the huge library of Tom and Jerry cartoons they owned. Many of them had a character, seen usually from the knees down – a "colored" maid in the home where Tom and Jerry lived. Her voice had been done by Lillian Randolph, a great character actress, but it was a racial stereotype... not the kind of thing TV stations wanted to broadcast in an era of civil rights.

Chuck's job: Reanimate those scenes and replace her with someone else. I wound up doing the voice of the someone else, an Irish maid who was just as much a stereotype in her own way. My husband with the name Donavan loved it.

Not long after that, Chuck adapted the great Dr. Seuss book, *How the Grinch Stole Christmas*, for animation and I was cast as Cindy Lou Who.

It took a long time to record Cindy's part for that one. I think it took fifteen minutes. Chuck hadn't changed since we did *Broomstick Bunny.* He liked the first take I did and didn't require another. My big disappointment was that I didn't get to work with Boris Karloff, who supplied the letter-perfect narration. But that letdown was offset at the prospect of getting to meet the Good Doctor, himself. Like millions of people, I was hooked on Seuss. He was an icon to the world for hysterical stories and ridiculous rhyme.

I'm afraid that when I did get to meet him, I fawned all over Ted Geisel (that was his real name) – and that was before I was even aware that we shared the same birth city of Springfield, Massachusetts.

Some little jobs create big memories. Cindy Lou was just a few minutes of work but I got to be a part of a production that meant so much to so many. People still write me fan letters about my minimal contribution.

Chuck continued to make wonderful features, shorts and TV specials for MGM, including another Seuss adaptation, the legendary *Horton Hears a Who*, for which Chuck Who cast me as Jane Kangaroo. This time, I didn't get to gush over Dr. Seuss. Maybe he knew I'd be there and stayed away.

In the year 2000, a huge-budget live-action motion picture was made of *How the Grinch Stole Christmas*. They were adapting that marvelous book but they were also adapting what Chuck and his crew of storymen and animators had done with it for animation.

Because of his deteriorating health, Chuck wasn't able to get out to a theater to see it, which was just as well. It might have finished him off, then and there. Unfortunately, I was well enough to go.

I called him after and spoke to him and his beautiful wife, Marion. I told them that I thought the motion picture was by far inferior to his animated T.V. special – too violent and unfaithful to Dr. Seuss. Chuck giggled with evident glee...a bright spot in his life. I'm sure I'm not the only one who told him that.

Hobe and I always said "Peanie Brittle" when we wanted a snack with a cracker and peanut butter, and I still do. We picked up that and so many brilliant jokes and phrases from Walt Kelly's great newspaper strip, *Pogo*. Little Pogo Possum loved peanut butter...or peanie brittle, as he called it. We loved Kelly's nonsensical mispronunciations. We loved all the colorful characters he drew to populate the Okefenokee Swamp, from Howland Owl to Churchy

LeFemme. They were all animals but you couldn't help but recognize all your friends and everyone you knew.

So when Chuck called and said he was adapting *Pogo* into animation, and that he wanted me to play the title character, my excitement flew off the charts. I was also going to voice the beautiful lady skunk, Mam'selle Hepzibah, which meant that I'd be playing a romantic scene with myself.

Best of all, I'd get to meet and work with Walt Kelly, who was coming out from New York to work with Chuck on the show and to supply the voice of the cigar-chomping Albert Alligator. Which was logical since though he was all the characters in his strip, he was Albert the most.

Immediately, I had a problem. Of all the Pogo books, all of which I owned, which one would I ask Mr. Kelly to sign? *Pogo? I Go Pogo? The Pogo Papers? Ten Ever-Lovin' Blue-Eyed Years With Pogo?* Hobe and I decided on *Songs of the Pogo*, our favorite songbook, chock-full as it was of Kelly's lovely lyrics. It was customary in our house every Christmas for Hobe to sit at the piano and play as we all sang...

> Deck Us All With Boston Charlie,
> Walla, Wall Wash and Kalamazoo!
> Nora's Freezin' on the Trolley
> Swaller, Dollar, Cauliflower. Alley Garoo!
> Don't we know Archaic Barrel
> Lullaby Lilla Boy, Louisville Lou.
> Trolley Molly Don't Love Harold
> Boola, Boola, Pensa Coola Hullabaloo.

A few weeks later, I shook hands with Walt Kelly himself and gave him the full Dr. Seuss treatment. Chuck directed us in the recording and even played one or two roles himself.

Afterward, I produced my *Songs of the Pogo* book and Walt readily autographed it with a sketch of Pogo, two hearts and the words, "I'm in toon with Joon," and he signed it, "Walt." Then he did something I hadn't expected. He invited me to join him for cocktails at the Hollywood Roosevelt Hotel, which is where he was

July 15/69

DEAR PEANIL BRICKLE FAN:

YOUR WORDS OF LAVISH PRAISE FOR OUR
MUTUAL WORK ARE CERTAINLY DESERVED.
THOUGH THIS MESSAGE IS BELATED, IT
IS NOT DIMINISHED, THANKS FOR YOUR
CLEAR SIGHTED JUDGEMENT. IT MAY
BE TRUE, AS SOME SAY, THAT YOU ARE
UNDER OBSERVATION FOR P. BRINKLE
ADDICTION BUT WE WHO UNDERSTANDS
NUTS KNOW BETTER. I ENJOYED YOUR
WORK AS MIZ BOOG, MISS MA'M'SELLE
AND POGO. WE ARE HAVING YOU MEASURED
FOR AN OSKAR.

LOVE...

A letter from Walt Kelly. He signed it with a drawing of Albert the Alligator
because that's pretty much who he was, cigar and all. © OGPI.

staying.

My first instinct was to decline. I'm not much of a drinker. Heck, when you're my height, it's sometimes a struggle to even get up on one of those bar stools, plus I was due later at another recording session, one for the *Beetle Bailey* cartoons. But how do you say no to your favorite cartoonist, especially when he's a sweet guy like Walt Kelly? I couldn't.

The stools at the Hollywood Roosevelt were high but they didn't match how high I got from one martini. Walt was so nice and such a fascinating talker that I hated to say goodbye to him...but Beetle was waiting. A kiss on the cheek and I was off to a studio, a few blocks away on Vine Street.

The role of Private Beetle Bailey was played by Howard Morris, who everyone loved from the moment they first saw him on TV, playing sidekick to Sid Caesar. I played Beetle's girl friend.

I've done hundreds and hundreds of recording sessions...so many that I can barely remember any one in particular. But I'll never forget that one, and I don't think Howie Morris ever forgot it, either. I missed lines. I read the other actors' parts. I started laughing and couldn't stop. We finally got through it, and I guess it turned out fine after the editors worked their magic on it. But as I think back, I'm surprised we aren't still there, doing take number six million and something.

So I have Walt Kelly to thank for the one time I showed up at a session drunk...but I have so many other things to thank him for, as well. There's an original *Pogo* strip on the wall of my home. I see it every day and I bless him for all his wonderful creativity.

Across the street from the hotel where Walt Kelly got me drunk on one martini, you can find the name of Chuck Jones on the pavement. It's part of the Hollywood Walk of Fame, where stars and filmmakers are honored by having their names placed in terrazzo and brass.

In 1995, when they had the ceremony to unveil Chuck's, he asked me to appear on the podium with him. It was such a thrill, watching crowds of people who'd loved his Bugs Bunny and Road Runner cartoons jam Hollywood Boulevard that day. I'll never forget the screaming admirers pressed up against the barriers and the police trying politely to hold them back. The roar almost drowned out Chuck's warm, humorous acceptance speech. That was the impact that his work had on several generations of cartoon lovers.

Around that time, it occurred to me that Chuck was more than overdue for another honor. I sat down one night and wrote the following letter to the Academy of Motion Picture Arts and Sciences...

In his autobiography, Chuck Jones recounts his father's favorite quote from the B.C. philosopher, Aristophanes. Well, here's another gem dropped by Aristophanes. "Haven't you sometimes seen a cloud that looks like a centaur or a leopard perhaps or a roaf or a bull?" Chuck Jones in the 20th century A.D. did. He saw a Road Runner, a Wile E. Coyote, a frog, all kinds of anthropomorphic animals, including a bunny – Bugs

Chuck Jones in his natural habitat: At the board, drawing something wonderful for somebody.

Witch Hazel returned several more times to menace Bugs. © Warner Brothers Cartoons.

by name.

Shortly after his being born in 1912, Chuck picked up a pencil with innovation, predetermining his success and fame. After studying at Chounaird Art Institute in his teens, he started his career as a cel washer for Charles Mintz, Ub Iwerks and Walter Lantz. From cel washer, to director, to writer, to producer, how did he do it? His being a classicist didn't hurt.

His joining Warner Brothers in the thirties won him his greatest fame in garnering two Oscars, which, of course, were commandeered by Warner's. When the Warner Animation closed it doors in the sixties, Chuck joined the animation unit at MGM directing several shorts including *How the Grinch Stole Christmas* and the Oscar-winning *The Dot and the Line*. He founded his own company in 1962 writing and directing 13 films. Three of Kipling – *The Jungle Book,*

Rikki-Tikki-Tavi and *Mowgli's Brothers,* all receiving Parent's Choice Awards.

By the way, he has lectured and conducted workshops at the Universities of Stanford, Kansas, Iowa, John Hopkins, California, Nevada, San Francisco State College, Art Center of Design in Pasadena, Cal Arts, USC, and UCLA.

He was honored by the British Film Institute, Kennedy Film Center, AFI, Toronto, Zagreb, Montreal Festivals, and is a Regent's Lecturer at the University of California at La Jolla.

He was a visiting lecturer at Cambridge University and Guardian Lecturer in England.

He has been bestowed honors by the Telluride Film Festival, as well as festivals in Deauville, Belgium, Toronto, Quebec, Montreal, Miami, Dallas, and Sydney, Australia.

He has received commendations for his contributions to children's causes.

At 83, Chuck Jones is still at it – back at Warner's writing, drawing, and producing theatrical shorts, as well as drawing original cels of his famous characters.

The foregoing is my reason for writing to you, The Board of Governors of The Motion Picture Academy, to request your considering Chuck Jones to be a recipient of a Life Achievement Award. He deserves it.

Well, Chuck did receive another Oscar in 1996. Not because of my letter alone, but those from countless entertainment film celebrities as well. That was the time that I had to take a compulsory year off, after nine consecutive ones on the Board of Governors at The Motion Picture Academy.

Damn it, I didn't attend the Oscars, but I watched at a restaurant with many of his friends and coworkers. We cheered, clapped hands so loudly when he spoke with such elegance and modesty, that it was a wonder we weren't ejected from the place. But then, everyone else who didn't know Chuck was enthralled. I was elected again for a 9-year period until 2005 and attend the ceremonies every year. But I truly regret my not being at the Oscars that year to pump his hand and plop a kiss on his cheek. Oh well, I had plenty more time to do that in the years to come.

Not long after, Chuck returned the favor. Remember that star he got on the Hollywood Walk of Fame?

Not everyone gets one of those. The Hollywood Chamber of Commerce only votes around twenty per year, and that includes performers in television, radio, motion pictures and the recording industries. Someone has to sponsor you and lobby for you. Someone also has to come up with the fee.

In 2000, I got a star there. Because of Chuck.

Late the year before, we were talking on the phone and I forget how the subject even came up. But Chuck suddenly realized I wasn't on the Hollywood Walk of Fame and that bothered him. "Mel Blanc has a star," he said. "You're going to get one if I have anything to say about it."

Chuck was in failing health but this seemed to get his blood circulating again. I later found out that after we got off the phone, he called someone at Warner Brothers and said, "It's outrageous that June Foray doesn't have a star up there. Get the studio behind it. Get her one."

They did. The studio had the clout. More importantly, they had the fee. At the time, it was $15,000.

Once it was official, Chuck called me, his voice ringing with triumph. "You're going to get a star because you are one."

It was a thrill but then a funny thing happened on my walk to Hollywood Boulevard. Universal Studios was about to release their movie, *The Adventures of Rocky & Bullwinkle*, with me providing the voice of Guess Who. Someone there thought, "Hey, Rocky's in *our* movie. We can't let Warner Brothers get the credit for June's star." And they went to the Walk of Fame people and demanded that they be the ones to pay for it.

I was flattered to have two big movie studios fighting over me. It was more delicious than having the two best-looking guys on campus wrestling over who'd get to take me to the prom. I'm not sure who wound up writing the check.

All I know is that on July 7, 2000, a nice crowd of people gathered up on Hollywood just East of La Brea. Stan Freberg was there. Steve Allen was there. Dozens and dozens of my friends were there. I was only sorry Chuck wasn't among them. He was too ill to attend so we had to settle for having him there in spirit. That wasn't so bad since Chuck had a lot of spirit, and he had it right up to the end. He died in February of 2002.

I have so many other memories of him, all wonderful. The one I think I'll use to close this goes with the sketch at the bottom of this page.

It was done in 1981. We were meeting for lunch to discuss I-don't-remember-what. When I arrived at the restaurant, Chuck was sitting there drawing. Although I'm naked in the picture, Chuck never saw me that way, at least in reality. Still, it's a pretty good likeness of me when I was young.

The sign between us reads, "June Foray Lunch," The writing at the bottom says, "To June. It's Jones in Jun-uwary. Love, Chuck."

I brought this sketch and my answer to him at his 85th birth-

day party on the 26th of September 1981, and the 17th of September 1997 – his 85th birthday. The audience enjoyed it. And here's what I wrote:

> One time when we were working,
> I remember you said,
> "You're such a lovely lady,
> and we've never been to bed,"
>
> I really didn't need
> A witty repartee.
> My homogeneous answer was,
> "You never, ever asked me."
>
> This point in time, ah, more's the pity.
> It probably won't occur.
> We're not the man and woman, Chuck,
> We used to think we were.

Ours was a pure, enduring and unadulterated friendship. It's not because we weren't virgins...just Virgos. Everyone who ever laughed at a Road Runner cartoon or reveled in "What's Opera, Doc?" or sang along with Michigan J. Frog as he warbled "Hello, My Baby" misses Chuck Jones. And I miss him more than anyone.

CHAPTER EIGHT

My Rocky Life

As with my career with Warner Brothers cartoons, it all started with a call to go see a man I'd never heard of. This person named Jay Ward had done a cartoon show for television (then, a very new place to do cartoons) called *Crusader Rabbit*, but I hadn't seen it.

Still, it had worked out well with Chuck Jones. So once again, I went to meet a stranger. This one, I was told, had an idea for a series and he wanted me to be in it. The meeting was set for lunch at the Tail o' the Cock restaurant on La Cienega Boulevard, a fairly swanky joint back then. As long as there was the hope for a series, it was worth my time. Besides, I wasn't about to turn down a free meal.

So, I handed my big, old Cadillac over to the parking guy and went to the Maitre D' explaining I was there to meet someone called Jay Ward. "Oh, he's already here," was the response. He showed me to a table where two jovial mustachioed men sat.

The one with the funny, handlebar mustache said, "Hello, Miss Foray, I'm Jay Ward and this is my producer/writer, Bill Scott."

I sat down and they immediately offered me a martini. "I never drink at lunch," I replied, "because I get kind of sick to my stomach. I'll have a cocktail before dinner and that's pretty much it."

But they insisted, "Aw, come on. We're having one." I relented.

They went on to tell me the idea of Rocky and Bullwinkle, a talking squirrel and moose in an otherwise human world. It wouldn't be until much later that I learned that *Rocky and His Friends*, as it was titled for the first two seasons, wasn't that different from Jay's *Crusader Rabbit*, about a plucky little bunny with his dim bulb but well-meaning large friend, Rags the Tiger. Even the format, short adventure stories with cliffhanger endings, was retained. By then, Jay and his partner Alex Anderson had lost the rights to Crusader in a bitter custody battle between themselves, NBC and Supervising Producer, Jerry Fairbanks.

Anyway, I didn't think much of it at first, but by the second martini, I thought it was genius! I don't remember how I got home that day, or even agreeing to do it, but I must have because a week later we went to a tiny recording studio at Capitol Records to make a demo.

Jay's idea for Rocky's voice was that of a little boy, kind of cocky. It was easy for me to decide on the placement of Rocky's voice, but I decided to add my own touch to it. Instead of Rocky saying, "What are ya working on?," I would read the line, "What

Bill Scott had been an animation gagman and producer...but on *Rocky and His Friends*, he turned into one of the best voice actors ever, playing dozens of roles including Bullwinkle, Mr. Peabody and Fearless Leader.

And speaking of one of the best voice actors ever: This may be the only photo in existence of me with my beloved Paul Frees. It's a little out of focus but then at times, so was Paul. Courtesy of Keith Scott.

are ya workin' on?," dropping the g's. It gave the character that All-American sound that he needed.

Rocky was very bright, always questioning Bullwinkle's veracity. "Are you sure about that, Bullwinkle?" He's also a bit belligerent. Not in a mean way, but he definitely stands up for himself.

In the studio for that first demo, we had myself and the wonderful Paul Frees. Paul had done lots of cartoons for MGM and Walter Lantz, not to mention a ton of looping and he was going to play the Narrator. At this point, they still had not cast Bullwinkle, so Jay just had Bill Scott read it, and that's how Bill became the moose.

Boris Badenov and Natasha Fatale were also in it and this was the first I had heard that Jay wanted me to play Natasha while Paul would be Boris. "Are they Russian?" I asked.

Jay was adamant that they not be Russian. "They're from Pottsylvania. Do a Pottsylvanian accent," he said. We had a good laugh about that, but of course, there is no such thing. I did what you would call a "continental" accent. This was during the Cold War and Jay didn't want to inflame relations between the two countries any more than they already were. In those days, you never knew. Maybe a cartoon show would push Khrushchev to the breaking point. As it turned out, it didn't help, because the Russians got mad at us anyway, thinking we were making fun of them. The other interesting aspect to the accents, is that while Paul, playing Boris Badenov, and I as Natasha are both supposed to be from Pottsylvania, we weren't really doing the same accent. Paul would turn the letter "w" into a "v", like saying "Vere are you goink?" for "Where are you going?", which I never did.

I still don't know how they chose me for Rocky, except that Bill Scott and Lloyd Turner, another Ward scribe, had both been writers at Warner Bros. in the Arthur Davis unit and could have heard my work there, or maybe Jay and Bill were Freberg fans and became aware of me through the radio show and records.

In any case, we did the demo and I didn't hear from them again for a whole year. Not until November of 1959 when I got a call from Jay's secretary, saying, "We're ready to go!" Just like that, out of the blue. I had practically forgotten about it.

We recorded those first episodes at Glen Glenn Sound on Seward Street in Hollywood near the old Walter Lantz Studio. This time around, they had hired the splendidly deep-voiced William Conrad to be the Narrator. In the first few episodes of the "rocket fuel formula-mooseberry bush" story, he gave a fairly subdued reading. Even Bullwinkle was a little more underplayed. But a few chapters into the story, Jay started to direct Conrad to pick up the pace. Every time Conrad would go faster, the pitch of his voice would rise, but Jay kept pushing him faster. Finally, Conrad balked, "Jay, if I go that fast, my voice gets way up high."

With a twinkle in his eye, Jay replied, "That's what I want!" Basically, he hired William Conrad to not sound like William Conrad. Only Jay Ward would have done that.

Also in the cast was Edward Everett Horton, the character actor, as the Narrator of the *Fractured Fairy Tales* and the inimitable Daws Butler playing all the princes, kings, wolves and little boys. In the *Mr. Peabody* segment, we had Walter Tetley, a veteran radio

That's Jay Ward himself on the left, Bill Scott on the right. There are no photos of Ponsonby Britt, who was billed as the show's Executive Producer. That's because he didn't exist. He was just a name Jay and Bill made up. Still, you'd be amazed how many people I met over the years who'd say, "I know your boss, Ponsonby Britt."

actor, as the voice of Sherman, Peabody's boy. Walter was a little person whose voice never changed, so he was able to portray boys late in his life, just as he had when I'd worked with him on the Phil Harris radio program. Peabody and Sherman would go back in time each episode and either meet a female historical figure voiced by me or a male one portrayed by Paul.

If it weren't for all the laughing, we practically could have recorded an episode in real time. Each session would consist of five episodes of one cartoon – five *Rocky & Bullwinkle* chapters, five *Fractured Fairy Tales*, five *Peabody's Improbable History,* and so forth. We would read a script through once and then record it.

A typical session would last no more than two hours. Jay liked to record late in the day, so the whole cast was always present for recording since no one had any conflicts, save that one time Freberg needed me. See the chapter about Capitol Records for that story.

Contrary to what most people think, there was no ad-libbing in these sessions. The scripts were so cleverly written that you didn't have to add anything. In fact, it would have spoiled the timing. And even though we had the writer, Bill Scott, in the booth with us, even he never changed a word.

I did have to be corrected one time near the beginning of the series. I read one of Rocky's lines, "Holy smoke!" and Bill said, "No, June, it's not 'Holy Smoke', it's *Hokey* Smoke'." Little did I realize how those two words would take on a life of their own. A catchphrase was born.

We did two seasons of *Rocky and His Friends* sponsored by General Mills and syndicated to local stations. Then NBC picked it up

Dudley loved Nell but Nell only loved Dudley's horse. Men have told me they identified with the problem. © Ward Productions.

and it was renamed *The Bullwinkle Show,* airing in primetime with two new features, *Aesop and Son,* which was similar to *Fractured Fairy Tales,* only with fables and *Dudley Do-Right of the Mounties.* I only appeared on *Aesop* when there was a female role, which wasn't as often as in the *Fairy Tales,* but *Dudley Do-Right* would give me one of my favorite roles of all time, that of Nell Fenwick, daughter of Inspector Fenwick, and the object of Do-Right's affection. The only problem was, the sweet Nell was more in love with Dudley's horse, Horse, than with Dudley.

These two features would add two more fabulous actors to our little stable, Charlie Ruggles as Aesop and Hans Conried as the villain who menaced Dudley Do-Right, Snidely Whiplash.

Also on *The Bullwinkle Show* were live-action wraparounds featuring a Bullwinkle puppet. It was during this time that Red Skelton called Jay claiming that Bullwinkle had stolen his Clem Kadiddlehopper voice and he threatened to sue. Jay's answer was, "Sue me! I need the publicity!" Red never sued.

The next show Jay produced was called *Hoppity Hooper* and I was only a part of this show because they reused the *Fractured Fairy Tales* in it.

After that, in 1963 came *Fractured Flickers,* in which I had a more direct involvement. This show took silent movies and added satirical soundtracks to them. Hans Conried hosted on camera and also interviewed a guest star on each episode.

Performing on this show was a bit more complicated than recording a cartoon. It was like looping, except the words didn't really match the lips other than starting and stopping when the on-screen actor's mouths moved. We would watch the film so we could see which characters we were doing and then we would record it.

Once again, on this series, Jay ran afoul of a celebrity. There was a segment called, "Dinky Dunstan, Boy Cheerleader" where we turned Lon Chaney, Sr. as the "Hunchback of Notre Dame" into the titular cheerleader. In one scene, he's swinging on the parapet chanting, "One, two, three, four, who are we for? U-S-C!" Lon Chaney, Jr. was furious and he confronted Jay. "You have diminished the stardom and talent of my father!" he ranted. But then, like Red Skelton, Chaney never did anything about it. Jay had a way of defusing these situations.

The show was very funny, but unfortunately only ran one season. It would be several more years before Jay got another series on the air.

In the meantime, he found something else for us and the staff to occupy the time. In 1963, a new cereal was introduced by the Quaker Oats Company. It was called Cap'n Crunch and Jay got the plum job of producing the animated commercials for it.

They took place aboard the Good Ship Guppy, with the Cap'n and four child crew members, plus Sea Dog. Daws would take the lead as the Cap'n doing his version of character actor Charles Butterworth's slurred delivery. I played Brunhilde, the girl child, while Bill Scott and Daws played the other two kids. The fourth child didn't speak. Bill would also be Jean LaFoote, the barefoot pirate and Paul Frees would be the friendly announcer at the end of the spot when one was needed.

Like Stan Freberg before him, Jay found a place doing funny commercials. By this time, there was less interference in the scripts for the commercials than there was by the networks in television.

Cap'n Crunch and it's many spin-offs, Cap'n Crunch with Crunchberries, Cinnamon Crunch, Peanut Butter Crunch, *et al.* were the mainstays and the commercials kept the studio afloat until 1967 when Jay sold another series to ABC.

George of the Jungle was formatted more typically for a cartoon show of the time. There was no host and no filler segments like "Bullwinkle's Corner" or "The Bullwinkle Fan Club." It was three cartoons, each featuring a different set of characters and each with its own catchy theme song.

George was the big, dumb ape-man, played brilliantly by Bill Scott. I was Ursula, his mate. There is some confusion because in the main title theme song, they sing the lyric, "Then away he'll shlep on his elephant Shep, while Fella and Ursula stay in step." In the animation, Ursula splits into a twin and two steps off the screen, dragging an unconscious George with her. People would say to me, "Oh, you do both parts?" The answer is, George was so dumb that he couldn't remember her name, so he called Ursula, "Fella",

Tom Slick surrounded by the women in his life. © Ward Productions.

but there was only one of them.

The middle segment was *Super Chicken,* in which Bill Scott starred as the Chicken and Paul Frees played his sidekick, Fred. I didn't have a recurring role in this feature, but appeared only when a female was needed.

The third segment was *Tom Slick,* about a race-car driver. Bill Scott, sounding very Dudley Do-Rightish, played Tom and I was his love interest, Marigold. There was an old woman character named Gertie Growler, but I lost out on that part to...Bill! Well, I can't complain too much with all the work I got from them over the years.

Only seventeen half hours of *George of the Jungle* were made since Jay went way over budget on them, but they were some of the funniest and best-looking cartoons the studio ever turned out.

After that, Jay produced three short pilots at his own expense. They never sold. There were talks several times of reviving Rocky and Bullwinkle, but Jay insisted on complete autonomy, something that no one was granted at that time. The original series came about at exactly the right moment. There was little to no interference from sponsors or networks and Jay got spoiled. Or maybe,

Jay had it right all the time. Who knows what *Rocky and His Friends* would have been like had there been a censor or a network executive looking over their shoulders?

The commercials carried Jay through pretty much to the end. The next to the last time I saw him was at Greenblatt's Delicatessen on Sunset, across the street from where the studio used to be. We were having lunch with Howard Brandy, Jay's publicity guy, and Jay was suffering from cancer and not eating. Having been a recent breast cancer survivor, I said, "Jay, you've got to eat to keep up your strength. I had to eat, I had to keep nourished and I'm surviving. So, you've got to eat!"

He looked over at Howard and said, "June told me I have to eat, so I'll eat." And he did, if only a little.

A few weeks later, Jay's wife Ramona, whom we called Billie, invited me over to see him. When I got there, he was lying on a stretcher in the living room. We talked and he still had that wonderful laugh. That was the last time I saw him. Just days later, on October 12, 1989, he passed away.

I don't need to say that he left behind a legacy of laughter. That's obvious. But I'd be remiss if I didn't say "Thank you" for allowing me to be an integral part of the wonderfully chaotic world of Jay Ward.

CHAPTER NINE

Bandini is a Four Letter Word

My brother Bert, a clinical psychologist, not only has an ear for patients, but one for music as well and he's written a hit song. It's probably not among the Top Ten in Billboard, but it's raising hell in the American Psychological Association. "I'd Rather Be Oral Than Anal" must have some significance for him and those in his profession, but in my mind, some people might find the opposite more attractive. Or for that matter, a little bit of both.

Let's face it, we'll all do anything for money. Well, almost anything. And a performer is no exception. Maybe his capitulation to Art for recompense seems more intemperate to the uninitiated outside of show business because of the monetary returns for seemingly little work, or talent, contributed. Nevertheless, residuals for commercials are now a fact of life and we're stepping on each other's faces to get them. So when our agents call us for a recording session, we don't question the product. Man, we just put on our wigs and split. And talk, talk, talk.

We all know homeowners are subject to the dubious delight of seeding, feeding and manicuring their lawns, and the Bandini Company is in the steer manure business. Ipso facto, a marriage of necessity. But you can bet your bottom straw of alfalfa that the Bandini steer manure company vie in their advertising attempts to convince the bewildered lawn caretakers that one's animal feces are far superior for little stalks of chlorophyll than the other's. Frankly, offal is awful whether it's in the bag or just released by its creator. But forgive me for my being prejudicially one-sided in favor of Bandini. You see, they paid me, and this is where the psychological clichés of being oral and/or anal intrude themselves. Announcing a commercial is most decidedly oral, while the product is definitely anal.

The association began one idyllic Winter/Spring day when Daws Butler, my fellow voice specialist, recommended my talents to Bob Colombatto, a particularly perceptive young advertising executive. What peculiarity in Bob's upbringing caused him to equate sex with cow dung has escaped me but it's quite a spectacular combination. I was sans agent at the time, so Bob put through a direct call to my home.

"June Foray, I presume?" asked a singing, merry voice.

"It is, and you do." I was young and flippant, too.

"Listen, can you do a sexy voice, as if I didn't know by just listening to you?"

I think that I just issued some sort of gurgling sound, which he bought immediately. Money and talent confirmed, Daws and I hit the microphone the next day. Good things come in small packages, an obsolete shibboleth by the way, since chemical and germ warfare, but you have rocks in your head to assume that it isn't a source of irritation when a studio sound engineer has to separate the tall actor from the short one with another mike set-up. Heaven forbid that any voice be "off mike." That's one of the reasons that I liked working with Daws. We were both teenie-weenies.

Word has it that its equally refreshing for the viewer or listener to be the target of intelligent advertising copy as it is for the actor, and Bob zapped it to us. We read the one-minute brilliantly funny dialogue, and then I moved in for the kill, whispering hoarsely into the mike:

"Bandini is the word for steer manure."

How oral and anal can you get? Obviously, the ludicrousness of it tickled the funny bone of the public, telegraphed it to the adver-

Here I am with the great John Cleese of Monty Python fame, from when we performed together at a concert in Santa Barbara. He has nothing to do with this chapter but given its subject matter, I thought he'd enjoy having our photo here.

tising clubs, and our modest little commercials won awards up and down the coast of California. Consequently, each Spring and Fall came the clarion call – time to spread the you-know-what on your lawns. Perhaps the ad agency on second consideration thought that "Bandini is the word for steer manure" lacked finesse, even after having clawed its way to respectability. So the subsequent tag became "Bandini is the word for fertilizer," and it has remained that way ever since.

Even the layman, through reading lurid screen periodicals, is aware that "instant Bandini" (a euphemism, naturally) is always hitting the electric fan in Hollywood, no matter what the tangent of the entertainment business. In this case, it was all to the good, and I became known as the "*hit" girl of advertising agencies, affectionately *j'espere*. This credit, plus records, animation, TV and looping prompted a request for me to co-host an advertising club luncheon with Art Linkletter. Art is always genially funny, and they tell me that I was too. The only crack that I remember follows:

"When I record for this product, I get over scale and all the Bandini I can eat."

There was laughter and a burst of applause that would have exhilarated even the *Star Search* producer.

The ad man works in mysterious ways his wonders to perform. It's no mean feat to drive from the downtown Statler Hotel to Woodland Hills with wall-to-wall freeway traffic in less than an hour, but within forty-five minutes, it was a miracle. Greeting my return was a glorious welcoming committee. One husband, one dachshund, two great Danes, and ten bags of Bandini dumped in the driveway! Not the itsy-bitsy bags, but the king-sized economy packs. And this time we couldn't blame it on the Great Danes.

We had just finished putting in a dichondra lawn on our new one-acre establishment, so we could afford to be beneficent and give a few bags away. Needless to say there were many takers who blessed the largess of Madison Avenue and the Donavans. It wasn't until the charitable deed was done that we realized that our lawn required more organic fertilizers than our dogs and one cat could provide, and more than the five bags we had retained.

Oh, the irony of it all. The Woodland Hills Nursery had to deliver five more sacks of Bandini at full retail price.

Moral: Never look a gift horse in the...er, I'll let you finish this one.

CHAPTER TEN

It is Better to Have Looped and Lost

The above words are lettered on a sign that has been gathering dust for years in the dubbing department at MGM Studios, Sync Room A. It's a good thing, too, that it hung on the particular wall that it did, because in sheer appreciation, I faced east, genuflected towards it and praised Allah, since looping had become a way of ife for me, and an extensive contribution to my income.

Actors are egocentric, that's a well known fact. Consequently, my hesitancy to explain "looping" comes from not wanting to bruise those egocentric egos or divulge trade secrets. However, I am aware that people not in the picture profession are now sophisticated and hip to show business vernacular – scoring, laugh tracks, videotapes and dubs...but looping? What the heck is that?

I'll give you a hint. It has something to do with airplanes, but not aerial acrobatics.

In this frenetic society of ours, airlines don't tend to ground their flights because Warner Brothers, adjacent to the airport, is filming exteriors. A company will attempt to delay a shot for noise, but eventually, that becomes impossible so scenes go forward without regard to whining planes, roaring traffic, blasting winds and mewling mobs. There is always the sanctuary of the dubbing room after the picture's completion.

In the insular quietude of a recording studio, the actor listens on earphones to his voice as it was recorded originally. He watches himself on the screen at the same time and re-records his dialogue, using his own voice and picture as a guide, resulting in an exact synchronization, we hope. Simply put, it will appear to the moviegoer like the actor's voice was recorded on location, but now it is nice and clear, free of the droning plane or screaming fire truck in the background. *Voila,* a perfect, virginal scene.

Why is that called "looping?", I hear you asking. Well, I'll tell you, oh, impatient one. In the early days, the portion of the scene where the soundtrack needed to be fixed was on a strip of film that was glued into a loop, wound onto a projector, flashed on the screen and repeated over and over and over and over and over. Hokey Smoke, did it go over and over! But it was necessary for the performer to be able to rehearse the synchronization and do multiple takes until it was exactly right.

The method used to of prepare the actor wearing the earphones was a series of three rhythmic beeps recorded on the soundtrack. The performer needed to start talking at the point where the fourth beep should metrically be. But now in the 21st century, the computer is your co-star.

The technology is called ADR (Automatic or Automated Dialogue Replacement). It's still the same three beeps and you still begin talking where the fourth beep would be, but now, the computer can put the beeps in anyplace that's needed. This allows the producers to replace a small part of a line or even a single word and they can change their minds any time they want, moving the edit points without having to go through the tedious preparation of creating the film loop. The audio engineer just selects the point where the replacement should begin and the computer does the rest. It can also instantly be played back in sync with the picture.

Without attempting to be euphemistic, what if the performance of the live action actor just plain stank? If they're not able to coax a usable performance out of the original actor in ADR, then all hell breaks loose in the casting department as they search for another actor to replace the offending dialogue, reading the same lines but simply giving a substitute superior performance. Occasionally, the actor on the screen is not available for his own lines to be looped and then they must find someone else who can match his voice to the original, a sound-alike. It took awhile to get to the point, but there it is, and here I am. Foray to the rescue. Help is on the way.

"June?" asked a voice on the telephone.

"Yes. Oh hi, Zyra." It was my agent's secretary.

"I have an interview for you."

Interviews, auditions or voice tests, if you will, still manage to impose a modicum of ambivalence on an actor. On the one hand, there is exhilaration at the opportunity of having a crack at a coveted job and then there is the apprehension that the competition will be too slick and too multitudinous. Ah, those cattle calls with varying degrees of voices and mammary glands! Cattle calls are auditions where the producers don't know what they're really looking for, so they call in just about every available actor in town. Thus, the waiting room is filled with so many milling hopefuls that they appear like cattle waiting to be slaughtered.

"Be at Columbia at 10 A.M. tomorrow, Thursday. See Bob Ellsworth, head of casting. He'll take you to Mr. Kramer."

"Stanley Kramer?!"

"That's right. It's for a movie called *The Secret of Santa Vittoria*."

The conclusion of that conversation, I admit, created panic in my little heart. Always having a passion for message-type movies, Stanley Kramer was my message-type guru.

The next morning, I breezed into the Columbia parking lot, waltzed across the street, complimented the girl at the desk for her new hairdo and wished I had been a little more assiduous in applying my false eyelashes. After announcing myself, I peered surreptitiously around the office for the other contestants. Strange...at ten o'clock, no other actresses.

Through necessity, no doubt, many a casting director is as cold as the proverbial fiddler's bitch, perhaps to prevent the impecunious no-talent from beating down the door of his inviolable asylum or to not convey false hope to the many who are called and not chosen, but Bob Ellsworth wasn't like that. There always seemed to be a fourteen-carat affection in his greeting. And today was no exception.

"I'll take you up to Mr. Kramer, now." And as we ascended in the elevator, he continued.

"When Mr. Kramer asked my advice on an actress for this looping job, I said don't look any further than June Foray. She's the only one whom I'd suggest."

That was confidence above and beyond. Flattering, indeed!

Introductions over, I seated myself, thanking Bob as he left Mr. Kramer's office. My eyes swept the desk and there was the latest copy of *Saturday Review*. I had just read mine the day before. Anybody who reads that magazine could have the first dance on my tally card any day. We were off to a good start.

He looked at me warmly. "Well, I understand that you're the best in the business."

My modesty allowed only a paraphrasing of Abraham Lincoln's famous speech, "I guess I fool a lot of the people a lot of the time, heh, heh."

"Here's what I need."

And Mr. Kramer explained.

He had shot the movie in Italy. Searching for authenticity, he spent several tedious months interviewing Italian villagers who could speak English, even minimally, and who could become actors under skilled direction. Humbling as it may be to the thousands of members of the Screen Actors Guild, it is an ugly fact of life that many actors are surprisingly adept in their first professional roles, especially when coached by the likes of Stanley Kramer. But still, this was a daunting task. Let's be honest and put the sabot on the other foot. Imagine how many people you would find in Tulsa who are bi-lingual above and beyond northern and southern Oklahoma accents. Nary a few, I'd reckon. Well, Kramer found his English-speaking Italians, and his patience and perspicacity paid off. The neophytes were sensational. Except in one case.

After the editing, Kramer felt that one old woman's accent was so thick that it was extremely difficult to understand, and yet, she couldn't be excised from the film. Naturally it would be insane and costly to fly back to Italy to loop her lines, with the end result probably being no better.

"Would you have a moment to look at the scene in our moviola?" he asked gently.

Practically flying across the desk, I leaped at the opportunity! Here was a chance to work with one of my heroes. After viewing the material, it turns out that the old woman was an utterly, delightful shrew, physically and vocally. It's no wonder he didn't want to lose her completely. More's the pity that her voice had to be replaced. For her...not for me.

"So you think you could match that, Miss Foray?"

This photo probably wasn't from a looping session but we didn't have one of those. I'm just at a microphone somewhere reading something for I don't know what.

Crouched over the moviola, I rendered an impersonation, determined that my enunciation, even with an Italian accent, would be above criticism.

"That's it. Great. Can you make a looping session Tuesday?"

Even if I couldn't, I would have. Don't ask me why, but we worked at the Goldwyn Studio instead of Columbia and for only a half-hour to forty-five minutes. Between takes, Mr. Kramer regaled us with distressing as well as amusing anecdotes of problems encountered on the picture with our Italian buddies.

My elation knew no bounds as I drove back to Columbia to sign the voucher and contracts. It's rather silly that I'm an old pro in the business but, obviously, still star struck. Hollywood was saddened when we lost Stanley Kramer in 2001. After I attended his memorial service, I realized that no matter how endowed we are, we are all finite – some sooner than others.

Looping is paid by the hour, so the only decent thing to do is to be punctual, something I always am. I had an eleven o'clock looping session at 20th Century Fox, which, for the uninitiated, is in what is now called Century City. From my home, the best route is the San Diego Freeway. Angelenos' definition of the word "best" may be slightly different from those of you in other big cities. When I say "best", I'm talking about a freeway that is always being dug up, repaired, resurfaced, pulled, mauled, painted and closed.

So there we were, my buddy the car and I, tootling along this so-called freeway, when suddenly, the right two lanes were shut off to traffic. "Be prepared," as the Boy Scouts say and when the traffic stops, so does the driver behind my wheel. But, not the dizzy broad behind me, who pays more attention to Alfred E. Neuman than the Boy Scouts, "What, me worry?" Sitting duck that I was, I heard a screech of brakes, looked in my rear view mirror, saw her coming and thanked the good Lord for my seat belt. *Wham!* Right in the bumper!

Here is what the scene is like when two distraught women exchange names and drivers' licenses after an accident: Cry now, cry later... and a little more after that. Notwithstanding, my pretty white Cadillac with the new concave rear end drove on the lot at precisely 10:55 and disgorged its nerve-wracked driver.

Needless to say, I flipped through that looping session oblivious of everything except my aggravated case of the shakes.

That next day, I received my paycheck for the Fox gig but it wasn't until six haggling months later that compensation was sent by *her* car insurance company. And to this minute, for the life of me, I can't remember what picture I did. The only thing I know about it is that Dustin Hoffman was in it, and I didn't even get to meet him.

Of course, I *know* what I looped in *The Only Game In Town* (an airline secretary), and I didn't get to meet Elizabeth Taylor, either.

My voice is all through *Bells Are Ringing* with Judy Holliday and Dean Martin. (So is Paul Frees and Shep Menkin.) When Judy as the telephone answering lady is talking to Dino's girl friend on the phone – the one who's upset that he isn't taking her to the races – that's me you're hearing. When Judy is talking to a little boy on the phone and pretending to be Santa Claus, that's me. When Judy's singing the song, "Drop That Name," you may notice that one of the actresses who sings along with her sounds an awful lot like Boris Badenov's lady friend, Natasha. Guess why that is.

But I never got to meet Judy Holliday or Dean Martin.

For the movie *Hospital,* my friend Arthur Hiller called me in shortly before the film had to be released. There was a scene with George C. Scott and Diana Rigg and something about her dialogue had to be changed. Which was a problem because Diana Rigg was in England doing a play. "Do you think you can match her, Junie?" he asked me.

"Well, I'll try," I said. "And you can decide if it matches. After all, you're the director."

I guess it worked because he used it...and don't ask me which scene it was. When I saw the movie some months later, I didn't remember and I couldn't tell. I even asked Arthur the next time I saw him at an Academy meeting because I wasn't sure if it had stayed in. But he assured me it had and that he couldn't remember which scene it was, either.

But as you might imagine, I didn't meet Diana Rigg.

Ah, but it's been different with Jerry Lewis, the looper's best-

Three actors who, in addition to their work in cartoons, spent a lot of time looping other actors in movies. At left is Daws Butler. At right is Shepard Menkin. Among his many animation roles, Shep played the great inventor Clyde Crashcup on *The Alvin Show*. I think this photo was taken when we were addressing a class of aspiring voiceover actors.

friend. When I was working for Capitol Records on kiddie albums, I met all kinds of beautiful guest recording artists, and Jerry Lewis was one of them. We made a record called "The Puppy Dog's Dream," resulting in a thoroughly rewarding professional relationship, whether the doghouses were Paramount, Columbia or Universal. Jerry has been a loyal friend and one time, I came through with him on a whistle and a prayer...but mostly the whistle.

For the most part, life has been good to me. Don't get me wrong, however. I'm not one of those perennially ever-grinning, nauseating, cheerful Pollyannas, but somehow that certain *joi de vivre* has always been a part of my existence. And that's why when I putter around the house, I whistle. Fun for me, but for my on-key oriented husband, sheer unadulterated hell.

My poor husband, Hobart, who happened to be a writer, (probably because he'd have made a lousy real estate salesman), maintained his office at home and was not only burdened by the responsibility of writing a well-turned phrase but also by having to answer my professional telephone calls.

I was slaving over a hot microphone at some distant studio, when Jerry Lewis' office at Paramount contacted my home. It was imperative that they know immediately if I could whistle. A wave of panic washed over Hobe due to the dichotomy of his emotions. On the one hand, he didn't want to lie, but his other hand didn't want me to lose the job. Somehow, he managed to stammer, "Err – she does character whistling, I believe." For you husbands, that is championship walking the fine line!

On the strength of that noble, defensive statement, Jerry hired me, and for the first time in my career, uncertainties in the hereto-fore-solid bulwark of my ability assailed me. After all, Jerry had not insisted on a voice test. This might be construed as a case of taking a job under false pretenses. Talk about the song lyric "I whistle a happy tune – and no one ever knows I'm afraid."

The half-hour ride from home was occupied by driving in a daze, mechanically, while whistling a happy tune to the radio an-nouncement with an exceptionally dry mouth. From the time I picked up my voucher at the casting office until my settling down in the rickety, old chair in dirty old Dubbing Room 2 at Paramount, my poor carcass started to tremble. The moment of truth had ar-rived on little flat feet.

After a cheery "Good morning, good morning, good morn-ing," Jerry said, "You see, June, in the picture, Connie Stevens is supposed to be wearing caps on her front teeth. They slip, and she's supposed to make a funny whistling sound. That's what we need here, okay?"

Was it okay? It was beautiful! There was more relief for me in that short bit of dialogue than Alka-Seltzer could ever afford. And my performance was credible and funny.

Since that fateful day, Jerry bought my looping on practically every picture he made, and when he left Paramount for Columbia, there I went doing *Hook, Line and Sinker*.

Not all looping jobs are fun. Some of them are rather sad.

When terminal illness struck Ann Sheridan, all Hollywood, not just those intimately involved in her series, *Pistols and Petticoats*, grieved and yet strived for a little bit of light-heartedness around this valiant woman with guts enough to finish shooting an episode, working until the weekend of her passing. Our town was losing one of its own, a pioneer, a super-star, but, more importantly, a human being of substance and quality.

Surely, the necessity for calling me to match her voice and loop her exteriors, the final only unfinished chore left behind, was painful and distressing. Rather than being ghoulish, it was instead, professional.

She would have insisted upon it.

CHAPTER ELEVEN

Vocal Girl
Makes Good

In 1959, about the same time we were doing *Rocky and His Friends*, Mattel Toys was introducing a new doll capable of saying eleven different phrases when you pulled the ring on her back. The doll's name was Chatty Cathy and I provided the voice. She said things like, "I love you," and "Tell me a story."

Then, in 1963, Rod Serling did an episode of *The Twilight Zone* called "Living Doll" that parodied Chatty Cathy as Talky Tina. To make it as authentic as possible, I was called upon to speak for Tina. She was a friendly doll, except to the father of the family, played by Telly Savalas. To him, she said things like, "My name is Talky Tina and I'm going to kill you." It was fun being able to do readings that went from sweet to sinister.

I did the pilot for *The Flintstones*, then called *The Flagstones* with Daws Butler. He played Fred and Barney and I was Betty Rubble. I guess the saying, "You can't win them all" is true, because I didn't end up getting the part, but then, neither did Daws. It would be several years before I worked for Hanna-Barbera again.

However, I kept busy doing voices for many other programs, like *The Alvin Show*. I was also on *Calvin and the Colonel*, a short-lived primetime show based loosely on *Amos & Andy* and starring the same two actors that had played them on the radio, Freeman Gosden and Charles Correll.

I worked on *The Famous Adventures of Mr. Magoo* and kept doing the voice of Tweety's Granny during this time, as well as working with Chuck Jones on his *Tom and Jerry* shorts for MGM and with Walter Lantz on the cartoons his studio was still producing.

Hanna-Barbera made a Flintstones feature in 1966 titled *The Man Called Flintstone*, a spy spoof. I was beginning to worry about being typecast because I played a female spy, Tanya Malachite, in it. Well, at least it wasn't a witch named Hazel.

In 1967, I did my final on-camera role, except for a cameo in 1992's *Boris and Natasha* live-action feature. It was a Hispanic telephone operator on the series *Green Acres* with Eddie Albert and Eva Gabor. I gave it up after that. It took more time and trouble than it was worth to memorize lines and sit around on a set all day waiting to film your scene. Give me the roll-out-of-bed-record-your-lines-in-your-pajamas-world of voiceover any day!

My voice continued to be heard coming out of dolls and radios and TVs and little kids on such shows as *Gilligan's Island*, *Bewitched*, *Lost in Space*, *Get Smart* and *The Brady Bunch*.

The seventies saw a spate of specials featuring Bugs Bunny and other Warner Brothers characters, often intermingling new footage with old. For the new, I got to reprise old favorites Granny, Witch Hazel and even Millicent, the overbearing rabbit.

Chuck Jones produced a couple of Raggedy Ann and Andy specials in which I spoke for Ann and Daws was Andy.

1981 found me as Aunt May Parker on the *Spider-Man and His Amazing Friends* series. The Eighties also ushered in my next long-running series, *Smurfs*.

Believe it or not, I had to audition for *Smurfs*. Originally, I read for the part of Smurfette, but I didn't get it. Gordon Hunt, the director, suggested that I try another Smurf. I looked them over and saw that they had this line written for the one called Jokey, "Hyuk!" So, I invented the Jokey laugh and that did the trick. I became part

Millicent bunny-hugging her huggable honey bunny in *The Bugs Bunny Diet Special.* © Warner Brothers Cartoons.

of a long-running ensemble that included some of my favorite co-actors, including the great Don Messick as Papa Smurf.

After a few years, they were adding new characters and Gordon asked if I'd audition for another part. I said, "I double and triple on practically every show I'm on. Why do I have to audition?"

But then I figured, what do I have to lose? The character was Mother Nature and I knew that up-and-coming actresses would

Raggedy Ann and Andy...as reimagined by Mr. Charles M. Jones.

walk in, see the character and think, "I'll do June Foray's Granny voice for this." I decided not to do June Foray's Granny voice. My idea was to make her kind of ditzy.

When Joe Barbera listened to the audition tapes, the readings were numbered so he had no idea who was who. He listened to Number One and said, "Naw, sounds too much like June Foray." Number Two was played and he sneered, "June Foray all over again." This went on and on, June after June, Foray after Foray.

He was growing weary when he got to number Twenty-Three. Startled, he leapt to his feet and shouted, "Now *that's* the voice I want! Finally, someone who isn't doing June Foray!"

It was June Foray. That's how I was cast as Mother Nature.

I continued working for every studio in town, Hanna-Barbera, Ruby-Spears, Marvel, DIC. I can't even remember all the shows. If they were making cartoons, they had to have Foray. I turned up on many an episode of *Garfield and Friends,* as well.

The Eighties culminated in one of the highest-budget combination animated/live-action films to date, *Who Framed Roger Rabbit.* I played Wheezy, one of the weasel gang. This was the last time Mel

Blanc would voice his famous Warner Brothers characters.

Disney also started producing animated series for television during this decade, meaning that they had to give some control of the animation to foreign studios, something Walt Disney had never had to consider. Their shows became very popular and I had major roles on several of them. On *Adventures of the Gummi Bears*, I was Grammi Gummi, but being on this show was especially joyous because I was reunited with my old friend, Bill Scott, who played Gruffi Gummi. I was also the recurring villains, Magica De Spell and Ma Beagle on *Duck Tales*, a show based on the *Uncle Scrooge* and *Donald Duck* comic books by Carl Barks.

And then, after more than forty years, I was back at Disney Features, this time with my feet untied. They had cast someone else to play Grandmother Fa in the film, *Mulan*. Apparently, they were unhappy because I got the call to replace her. Grandma was a feisty old woman, making it a very fun role. I even got to reprise her in the direct-to-DVD sequel.

In the nineties, Warner Brothers was producing cartoons for

Disney's *Adventures of the Gummi Bears*. I'm the third one from the left. © Walt Disney Productions.

Among the many funny folks I got to work with were Jonathan Winters (on *Smurfs*) and Gary Owens (on *Garfield and Friends*). The lady next to Gary is his wonderful wife, Arleta.

television and they decided to go with one called *The Sylvester & Tweety Mysteries*, starring the cat, the canary and the granny as detectives who solve crimes. It was still the same Granny I'd played for years even if she had taken on some of the traits of Angela Lansbury on the TV show, *Murder She Wrote*.

The big, disturbing enigma about Granny's new gig began one day when Don Pitts, my caring fabulous agent then and still, called to ask. "Would you audition tomorrow for Warner's?"

Audition for Warner's? I hadn't auditioned for Warner's when I got my first job there playing Witch Hazel. I'd done hundreds of recordings for them since. Why did I have to audition for them now?

That was my first thought but then I had my second, which was that this must be a brand new character. I asked Don what it was.

"It's for Granny," he said.

"WHAT?," I shouted. "Are you kidding? There's got to be a mistake. I *am* Granny." "Not for the producers there, you're not,"

Don explained. I didn't use the "F" word, but I did insist that Don tell them to go to hell. Of course, Don is always circumspect and obviously didn't advise the producers there to hit the road to perdition. I later heard they wanted Granny to sound more like Bea Benaderet.

Bea Benaderet! Bea hadn't done Granny in something like forty years. Almost all the Tweety cartoons they were running night and day on Cartoon Network had my Granny. That was the one several generations of kids grew up on.

I was depressed for weeks about this. It's bad enough to lose a job because they think you're too old for it. Can you imagine losing a job as a little old lady?

Finally, my telephone rang. It was Andrea Romano, the casting and voice director over at Warner's. I was happy to hear from her and even happier when she asked, "June, would you do Granny for us?"

I was flabbergasted. "You mean it?" She assured me that she did and they did.

What made them change their mind? Chuck.

Granny, letting Sylvester know who's boss. © Warner Brothers Cartoons.

Chuck heard what they were planning, called the Powers That Be (or Then Were) and asked, "How dare you cast a fake Granny?"

I don't know if that brought them to their senses or if they just didn't want to make the great Chuck Jones mad but Granny, the wily detective, appeared for years on *The Sylvester & Tweety Mysteries* and I later played her for the 2003 *Looney Tunes Back in Action* movie and for a *Baby Looney Tunes* TV series.

We little old ladies sure get around...especially with a little help from our friends.

In 2000, the moose and the squirrel made it to the big screen in a combination animation and live-action extravaganza, *The Adventures of Rocky and Bullwinkle*. Des McAnuff directed and Robert DeNiro (a longtime fan of the show, as it turned out) played Fearless Leader and served as one of the Executive Producers. Dear Bill Scott was gone by this time but fortunately, a worthy replacement had been found. Keith Scott (no relation) is one of the top voice artists in Australia...and an expert on the Jay Ward Studio. His ability to mimic Bill is absolutely uncanny, and when I performed Rocky's lines opposite him, it felt just like it had in 1959.

The year of this book marks fifty years since then, fifty years since Rocky and his antlered buddy first burst onto the scene. The movie reminded me, as fans do every day, how beloved those characters are over many generations. The influence is there in every new cartoon that comes along and doesn't underestimate the smarts and sense of humor of the audience.

Those who would "dumb down" their acts because the public isn't that smart, especially the young public...please take note.

CHAPTER TWELVE

Goal Posts

In 1957 in the town of Annecy, France, a group of animators founded the International Animated Film Association (*Association International du Film d'Animation*). The goal was to promote the art form of cartoons the world over; to recognize and encourage new and pioneering work. ASIFA, as it came to be known, was chartered by UNESCO in 1960 and branches began springing up in countries all around the globe.

ASIFA-West, the original chapter in Los Angeles, was convened by a band of distinguished local animation folks including Bill Littlejohn, Ward Kimball, Les Goldman and a few others. The goal was noble but for a while, the group didn't do much.

Whenever I traveled to animation festivals the world over – to places like Zagreb or Annecy – I saw cartoons treated with a respect they weren't getting in my home country. Even American cartoons and the men and women who made them were afforded a reverence overseas they weren't receiving back home.

That, I decided, had to change.

Blessed with a voice that gets attention, I put it to use rousing my colleagues along with the rabble. ASIFA on the local level, I argued, had to become more active. Nick Bosustow of UPA was then its president and I'm not sure if he gave in because he saw the wisdom in what I was saying or if he was just trying to get me to go

My baby sister Geri and me with the great science-fiction writer, Ray Bradbury. This was taken at one of the cel sales I held in my back yard to raise funds for ASIFA-Hollywood.

away. However and whyever, other members began to listen. One of my ideas was that there should be an award.

"They give Oscars for the best movies," I said. "And Emmy Awards for the best TV show." Right through the list I went – Tonys for Broadway shows, Grammys for records, etc. – before concluding my airtight case that there should be an Animation Award. It was Hobe's suggestion that we call them the Annies.

I rented a banquet room at the Sportsmen's Lodge, a big hotel-restaurant complex in Studio City. We had tickets to sell but also funds to raise. I got some studios to donate cels and we had a big cel sale in my backyard one weekend. All the proceeds went to ASIFA Hollywood, as I'd suggested renaming the organization.

The dinner, in which we presented the first Annies to honor Max and Dave Fleischer, was a huge success. Four hundred people turned out. We had more than that the second year to salute Walter Lantz and even more in 1974. That year, the recipients were Tex Avery, Friz Freleng, Chuck Jones, Art Babbit and (posthumously) Winsor McCay. And from there, it just grew and grew.

It wasn't until 1979 that someone noticed that all our honorees had something in common: They were all men.

The world of cartoons had long been a boy's club but not exclusively. We got to thinking: What woman could we recognize for her achievements? Among the contenders, one name stood out, that of

My dear friend Walter Lantz and I at one of the animation festivals in Zagreb, Yugoslavia.

Mae Questel, the main voice of Betty Boop and Popeye's lady love, Olive Oyl. Mae lived in New York and was thrilled at the tribute. She not only flew out for the ceremony but stayed with me and was she a marvel! Funny, energetic and truly wonderful. Getting to know Mae was but one of the many joys ASIFA has brought me.

Another has been watching the annual Annie Awards grow into a prestigious, black tie ceremony that each year is attended by everyone in the animation community. There, we honor the best work of the preceding twelve months. We also present the Winsor McCay Awards, which are given for a lifetime of contributions to the art of animation. That one was my idea. It was someone else's idea to also bestow the June Foray Award, given each year for having made a significant and benevolent or charitable impact on the art and industry.

You'd think ASIFA would have been enough to occupy my free (*i.e.,* not in a recording studio) time but no. In 1977, my friends Bill Hurtz and Tom Ray nominated me to serve on the Board of Governors of the Academy of Motion Picture Arts and Sciences, better known as the people who give out the Oscars every year. That's not all the Academy does, of course. It promotes all aspects of filmmaking and the preservation of movies from days gone by.

The films that often get the shortest of shrifts are the shortest of subjects. Bill and Tom needed an ally and advocate around to help promote the fine art of making short films...a dying art, some said, but one that still produces enough brilliance that it deserves to live and thrive. I guess they figured you need a short person to save short films.

At least four times during my time on the Board, someone has had the "bright" idea to save a little time on the Oscar telecast by not presenting those "silly" short subject categories. And at least four times, my allies and I have had to lobby and campaign and even campaign in the lobby to afford the makers of films of forty minutes or less, their dignity and opportunity.

My other big campaign was to have an Oscar category for Best Animated Feature. Bill Littlejohn and I started that one rolling about two decades ago. No one said no but the way they didn't

From the 1974 Annie Awards: I'm surrounded in this picture by legends of animation: Tex Avery, Chuck Jones, Friz Freleng and Art Babbitt.

say "yes" meant no. We had support from powerful producers, directors and actors. Gregory Peck was especially outspoken for the new award, and you can imagine how outspoken Gregory Peck could be. Still, it didn't happen.

It took fifteen years before we got around to "yes." The number (and box office receipts) of animated features had increased to the point where it just had to be.

The first Best Animated Feature Oscar was presented in 2005... to the movie, *Shrek.* Its executive producer, Jeffrey Katzenberg, was so thrilled that he called me at home just to say thanks.

Year after year, I was elected again to the Board of Governors. The rules require that you have to take every ninth year off so I sat out a few. But all in all, by the time I decided I'd put in my time, I'd served 25 years...and I'm proud to say they still honor a Best Animated Feature each ceremony and they still give out the Short Subject trophies on the air.

CHAPTER THIRTEEN

Shorter Subjects Than I

In the sixties, I worked on a TV show called *The Curiosity Shop*, for which a former UPA artist, Herb Klynn, directed the animation. Chuck Jones was the producer and he and Herbie cast me in three different roles -- a giraffe, an aardvark and an elephant.

The anthropomorphic giraffe was simple. She'd sound like a haughty, high-pitched matron. Those of you of a certain age will remember a character actress named Edna May Oliver. During her career, she appeared in dozens of movies and after she died, I cast her as a giraffe.

The aardvark, eating ants with his nose close to the ground, would make his voice low and gravelly.

But what about that elephant? She was a puzzlement. She was both a sweet thing and maybe not a sweet thing. Obviously, there was that overabundant poundage to figure into the voice and I thought briefly of Marjorie Main, the loud actress who'd played Ma Kettle in the movies. But Ma Kettle seemed a bit too harsh for the pachyderm who wore an adorable petite hat with a flower in it. I considered and rejected other approaches.

And then the thought struck me. A few evenings before, my

husband Hobe and I had attended a party where a slightly buxom woman in a high-pitched voice had forced herself on me, much as I had probably overpowered Dr. Seuss. She was annoying but she had a curiously melodic voice and I guess I made a mental note of it. You never know when you'll need a curiously melodic voice.

That was my lady elephant. The woman at the party had said she never missed anything I worked on. I wonder if she tuned in to *The Curiosity Shop* and thought, "Boy, something about that elephant seems so familiar."

Forgive my not remembering who was the producer for whom I was working. He asked me, "Do you know any actor who can do a Joe Besser voice?" What an affront to Joe, who was a star with the Three Stooges and in many other venues.

"Well," I retorted, "why don't you call Joe Besser?" Somehow, that hadn't occurred to him. And somehow, Hal Humphrey, a local newspaper entertainment reporter heard about it and printed my rejoinder. End of story? Not quite.

A year or so later, I was shopping for Christmas presents at David Orgell's, a local jeweler's. The fellow behind the counter had worked at KHJ during my Steve Allen *Smile Time* radio days. We greeted each other warmly while also exchanging Christmas greetings. Then he pointed to a customer with a familiar face. "You know Joe Besser, don't you?"

I didn't but we were introduced and he gave me a big hug, like I was his best friend in the world. "June," he cried, "you saved my career. I was hired for a big job I never would have gotten." We kissed, wished each other a Merry Christmas, and I never saw him again. But that happens a lot in this business.

One time, Hal Smith was hired for a cartoon. Hal was a sweet man with a voice for every occasion. The director came over to tell him which one he wanted and asked, "We want this character to sound like that old radio show actor, Frank Nelson."

Hal asked, "Why didn't you hire that old radio show actor,

Frank Nelson?"

The director replied, "We would have but he's dead."

Hal winced and said, "That's shocking. I just came from having lunch with him."

You'd be amazed how often that happens.

Hobe and I went through a phase of dressing up for costume parties. If you think we look silly, you should have heard us.

* * * * *

If exotic lands didn't beckon me first, after attending film festivals in Annecy, France, my return to home sweet home and hubby Hobart, would place me in Geneva, Switzerland, 40 kilometers away.

Chuck Jones was aware of my itinerary. He suggested, "If you're gonna stay a few days in Geneva, call my brother Dick. He's working at the United Nations. He'll show you around."

Well, I did call. My visit to the U.N. in New York was awesome. The one in Geneva would be equally or more fascinating. It was, and so was Dick, who bears a striking resemblance to Chuck. After all, they were brothers.

I had been feeling rotten in Annecy, with what kind of bug I don't know. So, after a captivating visit with brother Dick at the U.N., my return to the hotel found me disgorging the hearty lunch I shared with Dick. The rest of the day was a solitary one, in the bathroom.

By morning, what's that expression? Fit as a fiddle.

There was a charming cafe across the street that welcomed me for breakfast. I not only experienced a physical hunger, but a hunger for home engulfed me as well. As I dug into the *International Herald Tribune* and my scrambled eggs, I heard English spoken with American accents. "Hey, welcome home."

I had listened to and talked French for so long it was refreshing to hear our down home language. After paying the check, I had sufficient hubris to stop by the American table just to say hello and ask where they were from. Of the three, one was Canadian, the other two American.

They asked my home town. "Hey," said a lady named Beatrice, "I have a brother who lives there too. His name is Lou Moore."

For heaven's sake, Lou and Nellie Moore, my friends!

How can one explain strange coincidences like that. Lou and Nellie were just as astounded as I at the encounter. Serendipity? Fate?

Nah. Just Chuck Jones.

LOVE YOU

A drawing sent to me by the great magazine cartoonist, Virgil "VIP" Partch.

* * * * *

It was hot as Haiti. If Hell is this hot, I'll be a good girl for the rest of my life.

How did I know that it was monsoon time in India? As my plane landed in New Delhi, a taxi whisked me away to a gorgeous, exclusive hotel, up a hill and far away from the city. But I didn't want that. I wanted to be in town with a maddening crowd.

The hotel didn't mind my moving to another one in the center of New Delhi. After my checking in, I donned the coolest clothes from my suitcase and ventured out into the burning, busy street where I was confronted by an Indian gentleman. "What is your favorite flower?" he asked.

Without thinking twice, my response was, "A rose." And what do you know? He handed me one. Most Americans would say that, as did I. Thus, he was prepared...and rewarded with an American dollar.

When I thought about it later, I realized my truly great favorites are Gardenias. But never mind, he was thoughtful and a dollar richer.

Before my ordering a driver to take me to the countryside and the Taj Mahal, it was imperative to see the environments of New Delhi first. In the sweltering heat, my trudging down the busy streets was slow indeed. Slow enough to be accosted by a pitiful, crippled young man, belly prone on an elongated scooter.

"Ma'am, would you please buy one of these?"

I bent down and saw several articulated wooden cobras. Wow, it all came back to me. Chuck (Jones, again) had cast me as Nagaina (the snake) in his 1975 television special, *Rikki-Tikki-Tavi,* narrated by Orson Welles. Wouldn't it be sensational if I brought this wooden snake from India home to Chuck?

The poor Indian kid only wanted 50 American cents and that's all. Oh no, how could he sell it for that little? I bought two at a buck a piece. He was as thrilled as I with the sale.

A few blocks later and at 6:00, the rain was so hard that within minutes I was up to my knees in water. A book shop keeper opened his door. "Lady, come in until the rain stops." How kind and thoughtful. His invitation was accepted with alacrity, but the rain didn't stop.

After a half hour, with profuse thanks, I hailed a man-driven carriage about two feet from the ground to take me back to the hotel. It stopped raining by the next morning and it was off to Agra and the Taj Mahal. Shopping for family gifts was made expeditiously on my return. And the next day, the passage home on Air India was confirmed.

The plane took off in clear weather, which was comforting. It is sheer indulgence on my part, but I always fly first class. This was no exception. However, there were just about six of us sitting up front, my being the only American. It was dark and we were napping.

Then a flight attendant's voice came over the loudspeaker. "Fasten your seatbelts if you haven't already. We have weather problems."

I remembered that quote about "It's going to be a bumpy ride." All of a sudden, gusts of hurricane wind and rain jolted and rocked the plane, up and down, back and forth. We were flying over the Himalayas, a hell of a place to crash.

Very few things terrify me, but this did. If the plane was downed, what a horrendous death that would be. They'd never find us until weeks later (if ever) with the only American being June Foray Donavan, the Rocket J. Squirrel-Natasha-Witch Hazel-Cindy Lou Who actress.

No one screamed. No one uttered a sound. But panic was obvious.

After about thirty minutes of pummeling, the storm abruptly ended and the plane continued on a steady, normal course. It gave me no pleasure later when the hostess asked, "Do you know what AI stands for?"

"Yea, Air India."

"No. Arrival Indefinite." Now she tells me.

I landed safely back in Tinsel Town, clutching my baggage, which contained presents for Hobe, my sister Geri, her two daughters, and you guessed it, the articulated wooden snakes.

Mine sits coiled on my piano. I don't know where Chuck's is

now, but Nagaina and Ricki-Tikki-Tavi remain beside my cassette player to remind me of India, and of course, Chuck.

Roddy McDowall was an icon in the movie world even when he was a kid. So it was thrilling to meet him as an adult when we worked together on Chuck Jones' *The White Seal*, which he narrated. We later became friends where he joined us on the Board of Governors of the Academy of Motion Picture Arts & Sciences.

Anyway, we chatted amicably before recording. Then he asked me a personal question...

"Now that we're senior citizens, have you gotten your flu shot yet?"

"Nope."

"Well it's late in the season. You'd better."

That flu needle had never entered my arm or mind, but if Roddy said that it was a must, a must it was. So off it was to the Motion Picture Hospital in Woodland Hills, where I stood in line for a long time for that necessary shot.

What a mistake. Shortly after, I was never so sick in my life. If you've had the flu, you know what I mean.

After I recovered, my vow to never receive another was broken the following year because of the scare tactics of the press and physicians. Had the shot again. Sick as a dog again.

Never got another one and haven't had the flu. We miss dear Roddy. He's gone now, but not from the flu.

I live not far from Northridge, the city in Southern California that was the site of a rather large earthquake in 1994. It was a scary experience and many things in my home were damaged or at least dislodged.

When I went to pick up one spilled box in the garage, piles of scripts toppled out. I thought at first they were some of Hobe's from the *Lassie* radio show or something but they turned out to be scripts I'd written – my old Lady Make-Believe shows. I reread them and decided they were too good to be sitting in an old box in my garage.

Ted Turner, I heard, had been looking for fresh material for young audiences so I sent them his way. A few weeks later, his company bought them...for several times my entire annual income in the years when they were first written! But they never did anything with them and a few years later, I called up and asked, very politely I thought, if I could have them back.

"You can have them back if you pay us back all that money, " I was told. Well, I'd spent most of that money and sent the rest to Uncle Sam for taxes...so I had no intention of paying it back. I told the lady I'd wait until the contract ran out...

...and I did. It ran out. The stories are mine again. And Lady Make-Believe will live again. It's not going to require another earthquake to get her off my shelf.

It all happened fortuitously through my friend Mae Questel, the primary voice of Betty Boop.

Mae called me about a terrific artist who would love to have me record a witch's voice for him to be displayed in his horror museum. What a lucky lady I was that I consented to voice Zenobia the Gypsy Witch for Cortlandt Hull.

Cortlandt was a child of monster movies and the model kits that you could order through the rear of monster magazines. Not content to just build others' designs, he began making his own and eventually had enough to open The Witch's Dungeon, a museum in Bristol, Connecticut. The host is an amazing life-size creation named Zenobia.

Apparently, Cortlandt was acquainted with my original Disney Witch Hazel and all her descendants for other studios. I stole their voices for Zenobia, although Zenobia's brew contains a different concoction of eyeballs, mummy powder and shrunken hearts.

Mr. Hull charges very low admission but has managed to attract otherwise high-priced performers like Vincent Price, John Agar and Mark Hamill. Oh, yes...and June Foray. But then he shares his wizardry for art's sake and not for profit.

Whoever would have thought when I was a kid riding those gorgeous horses on the merry-go-round that as an adult I would continue around, not on horses but in an exquisite, Victorian panel painting by Cortlandt Hull?

The delicious humor in the painting is truly an "inside" joke. When Chuck Jones spirited me away from Disney to play *his* Witch Hazel, it was prestidigitation indeed. Cortlandt Hull's tongue-in-cheek painting of Chuck depicts him as a magician pulling a rabbit out of his hat, not unlike the way Bullwinkle often pulled Rocky out of his. But I'm in the painting as a magician's assistant.

It's exhilarating to know that Chuck, Cortlandt and I will still be going around together well into the 21st century on the Johnson City carousel in Endicott, New York. I caught the brass ring, nay – a golden one – since Cortlandt Hull was the artist.

Walter Lantz and his wife Grace Stafford (who was the voice of Woody Woodpecker) and I became very good friends. We were in Zagreb, Yugoslavia in 1972. (It was Yugoslavia at that time. Now it's Croatia.) Anyway, they gave me a marvelous Woody Woodpecker watch.

When I was coming home from Yugoslavia, I decided to go to Morocco as long as I was already closer to there than home. So, I stopped off in Algiers, Algeria. I was waiting in line to get on the plane but I couldn't read the Cyrillic writing and had no idea if the plane was on time. I asked some Arabic people, "Am I missing my plane to Casablanca?" and nobody could speak English. Then I saw a man sitting down. He was waiting to get on the plane and he was reading *Time* Magazine in English. I went over to him figuring that he was an American or could at least speak English and I said, "Have I missed my plane? I can't tell. I'm going to Morocco."

He was very pleasant and he replied, "No, it'll be here in a little while." I was relieved and as I watched, a black woman came over and sat with him.

As I was waiting to get on the plane, a pretty blonde, young lady asked, "Are you going to Morocco?" I told her I was.

She said, "I'm an American, too and I work with the embassy over here and I'm also going to Morocco." We finally boarded the plane, and we even had lunch the next day. After that, she had to leave and I wanted to go to Casablanca to see if Humphrey Bogart was there!

When I came home, I had the Woody Woodpecker watch with me. I had declared everything, so I assumed going through customs would be a breeze. The first man I encountered saw the watch and said, "Oh, I love Woody Woodpecker!" and he passed me through. I got to the end of the counter and two big men, one on each side of me, grabbed my arms and declared, "Come on, lady."

They took me into a back room and went through my entire baggage, taking everything out and going through it with a fine tooth-comb. After what seemed like an hour, one man looked at the other and said, "I don't see anything here." I was furious. I'm the last person to look like I pose a threat, all one hundred pounds of me.

It wasn't until I got home that I found out that the man I had spoken to in Algiers was an associate of the notorious Black Panther, Eldridge Cleaver and the woman with him was Angela Davis. Because I had been friendly and talking with them, the woman from the embassy had tipped off customs about me! It was crazy! You'd think I was a Pottsylvanian spy or something!

For reasons that will become obvious, I call this story, "There's a Horse in My Living Room." It's about how I wound up with a horse in my living room.

Still in our costume party mode.

The little girl next door acquired a horse after nagging her parents for one – no pun intended. However, I truly sympathized for Penny, a nondescript but charming quarter horse who had only a tiny stall where she stood, ate and eliminated for hours before being ridden.

"Hey Julie," I called over the fence. "Why don't you bring Penny over here before you go to school? I have an acre of land behind my house. She can run and graze all day." Besides my being compassionate, thought I, it was a hell of a way to save money on a gardener. It was a *fait accompli.*

Thus, Penny ate the grass and my lawn was mowed. When I wasn't out working, I noticed that Penny would follow my Great Dane, drink out of my pool and continue to neaten up my back forty. My dog and I had become very fond of our new part-time tenant.

Arriving home from the studio one afternoon, I parked the car and entered the house through my front door into the living room. Oh my God! There was Penny relieving her bladder, resulting in a huge pool of urine on my new, blue carpeting.

So whaddaya do in a case like that? You scream.

I did! I panicked and so did my four-legged equine friend. Penny beat the hell out of my living room, through the family room, the screened porch and out the back door, without plowing into the furniture or knocking over knickknacks. Her equestrian skill awes me to this day. Out came mops, rolls of paper, with my blood pressure hitting 190 over 80. Finally, the absurdity of the situation struck my funny bone. I poured a glass of straight scotch and laughed my head off. Well, the odor wasn't going to dissipate by itself.

So, insurance company, here I come. "Hi Hugh. I gotta problem." I explained in an articulate, but scotch-induced hilarity, about the horse urinating in my living room and will the insurance company cover the carpet cleaning?

"A what in your living room?"

"A horse."

A long pause on the other end, culminating in hysterical laughter. After he controlled himself. "Did you invite it over?"

"Yes."

"Then you have to contact the owner. We're not responsible."

The neighbors were not affluent. However, I could afford specialty cleaners, who I contacted immediately. "You clean animal stains and odors on carpets don't you?"

They said, "You'd never know that a dog or cat ever came near your living room carpet."

"Yes, but this was a horse."

Again, that long pause and uncontrollable laughter.

Well, they could and did. Penny's scent disappeared, but not Penny. She visited again everyday, barricaded from my living room by a closed back door and a much-too-small doggy door.

There was a horse in my living room, but hundreds of animals in my vocal cords. Squirrels, dogs, cats, elephants, aardvarks, skunks, bunnies, woodpeckers, giraffes, and, oh yes, a Warner Brothers Chicken called "Miss Prissy." There you have the nexus between the title and my voiceovers.

Hollywood has been scored and scarred in the basest pejoratives by cynics all over the world, perhaps justly so in many instances yet terribly uncalled for in others.

Still, Hollywood is people and what are those in show business but people – some conservative, some liberal, some moral, some amoral, some intellectual, some painfully less than that. The same ratio insinuates itself into every town and hamlet on our globe.

We here aren't any different.

And Hollywood's compassion is infinite. A minimum of 1% is voluntarily given out of every actor's paycheck in order to care for our own in the Motion Picture Country Home, and that's only the beginning. There are and were tireless efforts of Danny Thomas for St. Jude, Jerry Lewis with his Muscular Dystrophy Telethon, Bob Hope, Danny Kaye, Jack Benny, Frank Sinatra, Sammy Davis, Jr., the Paul Newmans, Burt Lancaster, Barbara Streisand, *ad infinitum*, for Biafra, Israel, Christmas Seals, organizations for promoting health, goodwill and racial equality.

Not just the stars contribute, my friends, but thousands of working actors, writers, directors, grips, film editors – even those at liberty – are Johnnies-on-the-Spot, joyfully donating time, professional skills, money and love to all causes worthy of compassion. Hollywood is a soft touch. And kind.

CHAPTER FOURTEEN

Old Friends

One of the downsides of being around as long as I've been around is that you have to go to a lot of funerals. Worse, they're funerals for people you knew and loved, so you have to be your best when you'd rather be home crying.

It is the curse of old age, one supposes. And living to say good-bye to your loved ones does, I guess, beat the alternative.

So I've delivered a lot of eulogies for beloved colleagues. Here in no particular order are just a few of them, the ones I wrote down and/or could find. This is the hardest kind of writing a person can do. The remembrance for Osama Tezuka was the easiest because I didn't know him as well, and didn't have to deliver it in person. I mailed it in. But the rest were rough. Sometimes, it's just so hard to find your voice...

Osama Tezuka

I often wondered why they called Osama Tezuka "doctor." And then I read his biography, which informed me that he had attended the University of Osaka and received his degree in medicine. Thank goodness he left the hypochondriac field of real live people for wonderful fantasy characters in animation. But then who knows if his study of medicine was instrumental in creating comic book and animated creatures with such finesse, deftness and creativity?

By the time that I met Dr. Tezuka, he had already produced his famous Astro Boy series and animated features *1001 Nights* and *Cleopatra,* let alone comics and children's books and concomitant political cartoons. After seeing *Jumping,* I was doubly delighted to meet Dr. Tezuka in Annecy, France. He was a modest, self-effacing man, sporting the perennial trademark, a Tam O'Shanter, although I doubt of Scotch ancestry.

Nicole Solomon and I were privileged to join Shiro Kawamoto, Renzo Kinoshita and Tezuka with their interpreters at the only Japanese restaurant in Annecy. It has been closed for many years. It couldn't have been our behavior, because it wasn't that boisterous. But somehow food engendered a glowing feeling of cordiality and affection, which obviously manifested itself over two hours of sake and sushi.

And then Dr. Tezuka with the brilliance of an international animator produced *Broken Down Film,* a typically American animated western, displaying typical American humor, an extraordinary feat, which endeared this talented man to us even more. Matsushita bought MCA, Sony bought Columbia, but Dr. Osama Tezuka bought our hearts.

Saul Bass

Whenever the name of Saul Bass initiates itself into a conversation, the reaction is, "Oh yeah. Didn't he produce those zany titles for that equally zany *It's a Mad, Mad, Mad, Mad, Mad World?*" Of course it was he.

However, there's much more. How about *Goodfellas, Cape Fear, Casino, The Man With the Golden Arm, The Seven Year Itch, Vertigo, Psycho* (including the shower scene), *War of the Roses, North by Northwest, Walk on the Wild Side, Mr. Saturday Night, The Age of Innocence, The Big Country, That's Entertainment Part III,* director of the live action epilogue of *West Side Story,* and the animated epilogue on *Around the World in 80 Days*? He did the special sequences for *Grand Prix* and the final battle sequences on *Spartacus.* How about that?

Hey, this is just a sample of Saul's work. He won an Oscar for the short *Why Man Creates,* and nominations for several more, but we all know that. But did you know that he designed graphic symbols for over 60 motion pictures including *Carmen Jones, Bon Jour Tristesse, Saint Joan, Exodus, Anatomy of a Murder, Advise and Consent, The Victors, Seconds, Grand Prix, Such Good Friends* and *The Shining?*

Saul himself would say, "Listen, you don't have to enumerate all of the trademarks I design, like Wesson Oil, Dixie Paper, Lawry's Foods, Hunts, Quaker Cereals, AT&T, United Airlines." Oh, well, the credits go on and on.

But let's talk about Saul Bass, the man. I first met Saul when I worked on one of his shorts, Naturally I had heard about him and his incredible talent. But I never expected such a kindly, enthusiastic, gentle and articulate person such as he. I was later to see him on a more personal basis with his wife and co-partner, Elaine.

I was delighted to eventually become friendly with Saul, the family man, when he, his wife, Elaine, and then 15-year old son attended the animation film festival in Zagreb, never realizing that we would serve together as governors on the Board of the Motion Picture Academy for many years until his death. But then, I never realized either that Saul and Elaine would be guests of the Shah of Iran regarding films for children.

I don't know how he had the strength, but it seems as though every time he missed a board meeting, he was off to Japan or London or Israel or Rio de Janeiro or Czechoslovakia or Amsterdam, lecturing, receiving gold medals and doctorates or conducting one-man shows.

But with all those accolades, Saul's greatest joy was the birth of his granddaughter. Forget his permanent collections in the Smithsonian, in Prague, Library of Congress, New York Museum of Modern Art, the one in Amsterdam, in Israel – he had a granddaughter! As Elaine says, he was unique and loving and caring – not only for his family, but for every person and cause.

I wish you could have seen him at the Academy Board meetings. He was untiring in his defense of the documentary committee in the short films branch. No one could be as literate and articulate as Saul, and he was successful in his dedication. Our meetings probably lasted longer, but we listened enraptured.

Let's not forget the exquisite posters that he created each year for many years for the Oscars. The design was pure Saul Bass and I'm so proud to be the owner of one signed by him.

To illustrate his thoughtfulness, in the last stages of his illness, he attended an Academy reception and made certain to wade through the crowd and express concern for me after my hip operation. Indeed, Saul Bass was a brilliant artist and a solicitous, caring man.

If you never met him, I'm sorry, but my life was enriched because I did!

Bill Hurtz

I worked for UPA and never met Bill Hurtz.

I worked for Frank Capra and never met Bill Hurtz.

I worked for Saul Bass and never met Bill Hurtz.

Then I started to work for Jay Ward and Bill Scott and hit pay dirt. I met Bill Hurtz!

I also met Pete Burness and never got a dinner.

I met Bill Hurtz and got a dinner.

Over a delightful period of many years, I also got to meet Mary Hurtz and Claudia, Tim and Ken over dinner at their home when the welcome mat was there for all their friends. They came to my house for dinner as well with all of our mutual buddies in animation.

And speaking of food, how many times have I enjoyed lunch in Jay's office on Sunset when Bennie Washam's home-cooked meals delighted the senses as one walked into the glorious aroma of cooking.

However – my first awareness of Bill's talent was on 7 November 1959 at Glen Glenn Studio when I recorded the Fairy Princess and the Witch for the famous (or infamous) *Fractured Fairy Tale,* "Sleeping Beautyland." Who can ever forget his comical likeness of Walt Disney?

Bill's direction on that short has become legendary. If that had been a theatrical short, it would have won an Oscar.

And speaking of Oscars, Bill was dedicated (with all of his work keeping him frenetically busy) to the Motion Picture Academy when he attended all the executive committee meetings as well as interminable screenings to determine who received the precious gold statue.

If that weren't enough, he and Chris Jenkyns flew to Jim Lentz's art galleries back East where they signed cels that Bill drew of Rocky and Bullwinkle pushing up daisies. What successes they were. Every time I visited the galleries, Jim would tell me what enormous hits these guys turned out to be with their fans.

But I think, when I look back on Bill's life, that what I remember most of all was his constant smile, his sense of humor, his gentleness, his generosity and love and respect for his fellow man. What greater compliment could I give this dear friend?

When I think of Bill, I am reminded of my favorite poem by William Cullen Bryant:

THANATOPSIS

So live that when thy summons comes to join
The innumerable caravan that moves
To the pale realms of shade, where each shall take
His chamber in the silent halls of death,
Thou go not, like the quarry slave at night
Scourged to his dungeon, but sustained and soothed
By an unfaltering trust, approach thy grave
Like one who wraps the drapery of his couch
About him and lies down to pleasant dreams.

Sweet dreams, dear Bill.

Paul Frees

Paul was a wunderkind, the most versatile of actors and quite likely the most enigmatic – until one took the time to plum the emotional depth that he harbored under the façade of jocularity, wit and a teensy weensy bit of arrogance. We hadn't met when he was Buddy Green, the song-and-dance man. But under the sobriquet of Paul Frees in radio, where I met him, we were all aware of Buddy's dexterity as a singer, night-club one-line artist, consummate performer and mimic.

What director needed Humphrey Bogart when he had Paul Frees? Why hire Ronald Coleman or James Mason or Eric Blore when Paul was at the call? I wasn't there, but Peter Lorre, who had been starring in a radio series was summoned to Europe for a short spell. Paul, having just recorded a comedy album with Spike Jones doing an impersonation of Lorre, inherited the mantle of Lorre's role. Naturally, the audience couldn't tell the difference. However, just before Lorre departed, he admonished Paul "Do me a favor, please. When I'm gone, take care of our voice."

The greatest disappointment in Paul's life, I think, was the fact that he hadn't been born Orson Welles. Certainly, he had the sonorous tones but lacked those six feet. But then, who am I to be telling another short joke?

On camera, we performed together for thirteen weeks with Jonnny Carson on Johnny's first television show for CBS, *Carson's Cellar*, clowning, breaking up, laughing into the dissolve. And, ah, those loverly hours on end when we worked with Stan Freberg on his albums at off-the-wall times of the day and night.

Obviously, all of us who were voice actors spent inordinate numbers of days at the now-defunct Radio Recorders. On a certain session when I was recording alone, the engineer said, "June, I've got a $10 bet going with an advertising executive. He said that at one time you were one of Paul Frees' five wives. I said that you weren't. Who was correct?"

Well, I don't know whether or not my singleness between marriages was ever synchronous with Paul's but that engineer was ten bucks richer that day.

My most treasured recollections of Paul as a person and not just another fellow actor, of course, relate to the *Bullwinkle* show. We were a congenial, convivial bunch of people – in the prime of our youth – who learned to love each other, cherish and respect each other's talents, and opinions. We were family who ripened and matured together.

The ingredients of the hysterical, historical series were, Jay Ward – Mr. Big – the director and producer; Bill Scott (bless him), writer-producer and the voice of Bullwinkle; Bill Conrad, our intrepid narrator; Daws Butler, actor extraordinaire, Hans Conried, Walter Tetley, Edward Everett Horton and I.

Hardly a session occurred when we started the show (first at Glen Glenn Studios, then at TV Recorders) that Paul didn't sashay in as Buddy Green, tap-dancing, joking and singing his way into our hearts. The true affection of innumerable years between Bill Conrad and Paul manifested itself hilariously by constant ragging, taunting and teasing – convulsing us all in paroxysms of laughter.

The mirth simply had to have extended recording time by hours over the years, but who cared? Certainly not Jay Ward, who paid the freight. Every session was a party. Recording seemed incidental. In my mind's eye, I can visualize Paul at the table with his own microphone being the "choir master," "the cheerleader," with tongue-in-cheek, ingratiating sycophancy, asking Mr. Big if he, Paul, had controlled the actors to his satisfaction.

As you know, Paul was the synthesis of the well-groomed man-about-town. Yet under that sartorial resplendency and lordly manner, Paul was astride a white charger...an incurable romantic prince, searching, searching for the rainbow and the princess. No one really knows if he ever found them. I hope he did.

He deserved them. We have seen him cry unabashedly at the loss of a dear friend. We have seen his wallet emptied for those less fortunate in life than he. We have seen his son Freddie and daughter Sabrina, sources of infinite gratification. Paul had a sweetness about him, and my speculation is that he was a sensitive, insecure little boy inside that wrapping of Brooks Brothers suits and monumental talent.

A short time ago, after watching a particularly uproarious *Bullwinkle* segment, I was stunned again by Paul's phenomenal artistry and felt compelled to telephone him in Tiburon to tell him so. Here was a mid-western American, playing a Russian playing a Texan. A remarkable, exquisitely funny performance. Unmercifully, Ma Bell kept ticking off those message units for almost an hour. But words – simply tumbled out uncontrollably while we reminisced, laughed and cried. He was profoundly appreciative of the fact that I was a fan as much as a friend.

Well, Boris dollink, you are up there with Moose, and I am down here with Squirrel. An ironic Bullwinkle episode, isn't it? Our cast has been diminished Paul, but we're with each other forever on celluloid – and in our hearts.

With Bill Scott, the voice (and heart) of Bullwinkle J. Moose.

Bill Scott

It was nigh unto 45 years ago. Eternity being so infinite, 45 years seemed preposterously fleeting and finite. Bill Scott invalidated time and in that span, insinuated into the public and our consciousness, his wit, talent and ingratiating charm. Studio E at Capitol Records was barely bigger than a bread box, scarcely larger than a phone booth but roomy enough to accommodate three trusty actors, plus Jay Ward.

Two of the actors knew each other: Paul Frees and June Foray. The third was a jocular, young Bill Scott, whom we subsequently discovered to be the head writer and co-producer of *Rocky and His Friends.* A network later, it became *The Bullwinkle Show.* It was a pilot back there in 1958, and we all know what happens to most pilots, don't we? Relegated to an inactive file in a great network in the sky.

And Lordy, Lordy, what a hilarious *Rocky and His Friends* segment that was. Frees assumed the role of Boris and narrator. Shortly after that, William Conrad took over that latter role. June Foray did Rocket J. Squirrel and Natasha, and Bill Scott voiced Bullwinkle. Who would have thought that an inept anthropomorphic moose could be imbued with sensitivity and almost intelligent credibility?

Well, Bill Scott did.

Who would have imagined that a hopelessly idiotic Canadian Mountie could be adored by anybody besides simple Nell?

Bill Scott did.

Obviously, writing and subsequently vocal delineations transcended the ordinary and expected. He transported us into the halcyon never-never land of delicious fantasy and utter absurdity. This didn't preclude, however, his taking wagging swipes at the foibles of the real establishment with a paucity of words, an impish grin and a verbal dagger to the heart.

Then there was the inordinately gentle, compassionate and generous Bill Scott. His time, wallet and energy became the perquisites of students, social and professional contraires, anyone who needed help. He was the magic touch. The International Animated Film Society depended on his drollery and magnanimity as president and as a performer/writer at the animation art sales.

On our personal appearance tours in Boston, Chicago, San Francisco or various universities, amenable Bill was tireless in answering questions and would sign autographs endlessly. Yes, the recipients of his largess constituted a monumentally long list indeed.

He was a consummate writer, actor, singer, director, family man, churchgoer, human being. He's a part of our lives and our hearts, and fortunately, he is on film forever. Boris and Natasha were always admonished by Fearless Leader – also played by Bill – to get Moose and Squirrel. But they never did, really. And they haven't now. Moose and Bill are just in upsidasium.

Jay Ward

How do I even start or finish stories about Fearless Leader, dollinks?

At the beginning, I guess. In 1958, my agent called me to say that a man called Jay Ward wanted to take me to lunch. Never heard of him. "Well, you might be interested in some thoughts he has about an animated television series."

At the Tail o' the Cock on La Cienega, I met a jovial, rotund man with an enormous walrus moustache, who laughed constantly as he related his concept of an inept Bull Moose and a trustworthy, loyal, helpful, friendly, courteous, kind, obedient, cheerful, thrifty, brave and clean flying squirrel. After the second martini, I thought it was one helluvan idea.

Within two weeks, the brilliant Jay had commandeered the brilliant writer Bill Scott and the voice of Bullwinkle, Paul Frees (Boris) and me. And with Jay in the booth in the tiniest studio Capitol ever built, we recorded one of the most gleeful pilots in the annals of television. As you are obviously aware, most pilots are relegated to that great sound stage in the sky, and I dismissed it.

After a year, my agent called and said, "Remember that fellow who produced the moose and squirrel pilot? Well, they're ready to go." Thus, in 1959, Jay Ward – this inventive, innovative man who valued humor as the essence of existence, created the most sophisticated, satirical, mordantly witty animated series ever to grace our screens.

My heart is heavy with Jay's passing, but my memories are tripping the light fantastic.

I remember Jay's patience, his laughter when actors became hysterical reading the scripts, ragging each other because whatever made US laugh made Jay laugh, and obviously, vice versa. He was fiercely determined, but he taught us all the ability to laugh at ourselves.

I remember when he couldn't sell his later pilots – the hilarious *Fang the Wonder Dog, Hawkear* and *The Stupor Bowl*, he said, "CBS dislikes us, NBC hates us and ABC detests us!"

I remember when we all flew to New York where Jay rented a train, which took us to Coney Island for the rides. Sadly, it rained on his parade. However, we repaired to the elegance of the Plaza Hotel where it rained box lunches and 40 proof hilarity.

I remember how Jay laughed when Paul Frees sashayed into the studio as the song and dance man, Buddy Green. I remember Jay's affable welcome to three or four of Paul's wives, when they attended our sessions…at different times, of course.

I remember when I asked Jay if I could change the voices of the princesses in *Fractured Fairy Tales*. It was always, "Do the Brooklyn, do the Brooklyn." It was always, "Do the Marjorie Main" for the Fairy Godmothers. He was always right.

I remember his little kids, and Bill Scott's kids and Paul's kids coming to watch their fathers work.

I remember going to the racetrack with Jay and his wife Billie to watch his horses run. Jay admonished my husband, "Don't bet on my horses." But Hobart felt obligated through his fondness for Jay to do just the opposite. He lost a bundle.

I remember how through Jay's influence with the city fathers, blocks on Sunset Boulevard were barricaded to dedicate the statue of Bullwinkle and Rocky in front of his office. It was his west coast answer to the Statue of Liberty.

Whenever I go domestically or around the world, the frenetic fans' favorite phase, as though they rehearsed it in unison, is "I grew up with you!" And so they did. But I am reminded that Jay and Bill Scott and Paul Frees and Daws Butler and Bill Conrad and I also grew up together. We were young. We were family. We saw the kids mature and became aware over the years of our infirmities and encroaching wrinkles, but guess what is forever young and fresh and vibrant? We all know.

Who will ever forget, "Watch me pull a rabbit out of my hat?" Or "Get moose and squirrel?" Or "Here's something we hope you'll really like?" Or the brilliant but insufferable puns?

Years after Jay said, "It's a wrap" at our last recording session, it has been a wrap for Jay and Bill Scott and Daws and Paul and Hans Conried, Walter Tetley, Edward Everett Horton and Charlie Ruggles. However. Jay's impudence will endure and titillate audiences well into our forthcoming century. As Bill Scott always said, "We have corrupted a new generation even now."

But I'm certain that if you look and listen intently enough, you will see and hear Jay still laughing at the Dudley Do-Right Emporium. There's a refreshing continuum of Jay in his children, Ron, Tiffany and Carey, and his vibrant, invincible wife Billie.

I've reiterated to Jay Ward over a period of years until just a couple weeks ago, my affection for him and how privileged I was to be one of the components in his *Bullwinkle, George of the Jungle, Fractured Flickers,* Cap'n Crunch commercials and his closely knit family of friends. I'm glad that I had that second martini at the Tail o' the Cock.

Alley Oop, Jay.

Epilogue

When Mark and Earl asked me if I wanted to dedicate this book to anyone, the answer was obvious. Some answers just are. I wanted to dedicate it to Hobe.

He passed away in 1976, the love of my life 'til the very end and beyond that, to this day. Since then there have been others but not in the same sense, of course. There have been the family members, the friends, the fans, the co-workers. I'm sure I said it a hundred different ways in the text but I'll say it again here: I really have been blessed to know an extraordinary number of talented, loving people.

You out there who read this book...you're probably somewhere in that list. It has been so gratifying to meet you, to hear from you, to just know that what I did in those little, windowless rooms in front of a microphone reached someone. If a show or film I worked on inspired you to write or draw or act or create, wonderful. If it made your childhood a little happier and therefore a little easier to struggle through, terrific. And if all it did was give you a giggle now and then, fine. Everyone deserves a giggle now and then.

As noted, I've played an awful lot of witches...so many that directors sometimes expect me to show up for a recording session by dismounting a broom and leaving it outside, double-parked. For the most part, they've been nice witches; only once in a while, the kind that tries to shove small children into ovens or, these days, convection microwaves. Some have been dotty. Some have been sly. Some have even been kind of cute in their own, witchy ways. There was a *Fractured Fairy Tale* – you may recall it – where one who seemed quite unlike a witch was asked how she'd worked some womanly magic. She grinned and replied, "There's a little of the witch in all us girls."

That's one way of looking at it. Another is that there's a little magic in all of us, male or female. We may not always know how to tap into it, to turn it to our and the world's advantage but it's there. You just have to know where to look for it. And if you don't, you have to look harder.

I think I found mine at a microphone. Yours may be even closer and might not even plug into the wall.

There are some, I know, who don't see it that way. They think it'll come to them and they'd better stay put in one place so it'll know where to find them...and you can try that. You can skip the study and not bother with the hard work. You can just wait for your dream to walk up, find you and tell you what it is. You can even be selfish and not lift a finger to help yourself, let alone anyone else. You can try it that way if you like.

But as a certain Flying Squirrel once said: "That trick never works."

Whatever I've achieved, I made happen. I got Lady Make-Believe on the air, I made the phone calls to get extra work, I haunted the lobbies of the radio stations, I even helped to get the Academy to award the Best Animated Feature. I don't mean to sound like St. June, but more the encouraging Granny.

The best I can hope for you, dear readers and friends, is a bright future and that you wake up every morning with that certain beloved Squirrel's other words bouncing around your skull...

"And now here's something we hope you'll really like!"

June Foray
July, 2009

CPSIA information can be obtained
at www.ICGtesting.com
Printed in the USA
LVOW13s0323090817
544326LV00016B/538/P

9 781593 934613